Children and Themes

A teacher's guide to
creative work

Alan M. Lynskey
Headmaster, Greenbank School, Rochdale

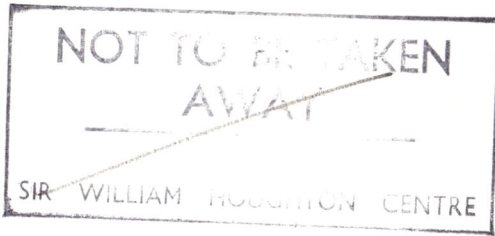

Oxford University Press

Oxford University Press, Ely House, London W.1

OXFORD LONDON GLASGOW NEW YORK
TORONTO MELBOURNE WELLINGTON CAPE TOWN
IBADAN NAIROBI DAR ES SALAAM LUSAKA ADDIS ABABA
KUALA LUMPUR SINGAPORE JAKARTA HONG KONG TOKYO
DELHI BOMBAY CALCUTTA MADRAS KARACHI

© Oxford University Press 1974

First published 1974
Second impression 1976

To Margaret, Helen, and Anne

Printed in Great Britian by
J. W. Arrowsmith Ltd. Bristol, England.

Contents

Introduction

All the themes in this book have been used over a number of years in schools where I have worked. The collection of references was being built up for some time before I set them down in this form for my present school, which is a primary school of some 400 children in a mixed middle- and working-class district. At the time of working out these themes, the building comprised a number of small classrooms opening into a central hall. All physical education, movement/drama, and music, and a great deal of art, took place in the hall, which was also the main thoroughfare of the school. Physical conditions were therefore far from ideal for thematic work, although the L.E.A. has been generous in the provision of books and audio-visual material.

As a school we were moving more and more toward the integration of subject disciplines and the widening of children's experience around a central idea. My work along these lines convinced me that we were working in the right direction in gathering source material, harnessing it for our particular needs, and developing further ideas with the children when their involvement was secure. But a structure around which to work was lacking, and at times this was a disadvantage. The reasons and objectives for taking a certain course of action must always be clear to the teacher, and a goal in the short term must be in his sight if he is to progress beyond the immediate. But the need to know the final aim of any work, and have it clearly stated, is also tremendously important, especially for young teachers. They can then be encouraged to branch out on their own, secure in their foundation, without the insecurity of the constant questions 'Where do I go from here?', or 'What do I do tomorrow?' This need must be evident in all new departures in teaching method. Unless these questions are answered and goals are clarified, I doubt if any lasting good will come of thematic work. So I talked with many teachers and, with much help, wrote out these themes.

The themes in this book were not then, and are not now, intended to be restrictive. For the sake of immediacy and economy I have written some of

Part II as if addressing the children directly, thereby showing how I myself activate the ideas. I hope this will be of use to teachers beginning dramatic work, who will be able to use these words initially as a base to work from. Indeed, any teacher, floundering as we all do from time to time, may find it useful to have these phrases to fall back on. This is not, however, a class book but a source book for students and teachers. I hope that those who read it will be encouraged to implement the ideas in their own style and idiom, will look for material of their own, use their individual expertise, and develop the themes in that light. They are intended as a basis on which to build, and I hope no one is tempted to simply 'follow the book'.

The book is intended for teachers in primary and middle schools, but within this wide range the appropriateness of the work to the child must be left entirely to the judgement of the teacher. Nor are the themes arranged in any order of progression. Common sense is the only possible guide, in the matter of selection from the material and in its development, on the part of teachers and students who read this and want to make a start in thematic teaching.

The starting is the vital thing, and I grow increasingly sure that it is the lack of adequate source material, and also an uncertainty about movement/drama, that holds back teachers who would otherwise like to begin. It is because of this particular uncertainty that I have concentrated on movement/drama almost exclusively in the themes that follow. Every theme, however, can be used in a variety of ways—to include art and craft, research, or observation. I have specified, in relation to a couple of themes, the particular forms that art and craft, and also investigation, can take, and in the introductions to the themes I have frequently given general indications of where work other than drama and writing would be useful. I have never felt that teachers had any difficulty in weaving work in the humanities, particularly history and geography, into themes. Any dicusssion with teachers has always immediately made the inclusion of these subjects obvious, and the specific inclusions have always been a matter of personal choice and inclination. In fact an awareness of how far themes can be extended into humanities can be dangerous. In striving for a balance of curriculum matter in children's work, and wishing to include as many of our traditional 'subjects' as possible, a theme can easily become distorted to include subjects that are not strong enough to make an impact in the context of a particular theme. This is particularly so when new 'teams' are starting, all very conscious of their own specialism. The danger will be avoided if the children's work is looked at from a long term point of view, and, if the teacher feels that some subject has been neglected for too long, then the next theme chosen should cater strongly for that omission. Though it is desirable that children have some 'history', some 'geography', some 'nature study', and so on, it is not at all desirable that each of these has a place in each theme. Obviously then, in selection from and development of the material, the initiative *must* remain with the teacher, students, and children using it.

It is worthwhile mentioning now that none of the teachers in my school use these themes, or others I have written. They all prefer to develop their own on a co-operative basis. The lesson is that they are now confident of their ability to do so. So, too, with this book: the teacher who fully adopts the methods it advocates will soon be independent of the book itself.

A. M. Lynskey
Rochdale, 1973

Part 1   Teaching with themes

Teachers and Themes

Teachers and themes

I consider a theme to be an area of experience which we share with a class over a period of time, say half a term. The exploration of this area will involve many subjects and activities, amongst them literature, talking, drama, art, writing, and music. Through these approaches we aim to involve the child in a rich, integrated area of experience, making it real for him at some point so that personal, creative work can arise. In my view, because this point of reality or identification is different for every child, the variety of approach in thematic teaching provides more possibility for the work being sharply realized and profoundly felt than if a single avenue of exploration were used. It is, however, essential that these different approaches are centred on one area, not directed at isolated topics. This treatment of one subject through a variety of media is, to my mind, the core of 'integration'.

Since such work will demand group collaboration and sharing of experience, children will discover through it the need to communicate and will develop some of the necessary skills. There is a continuous interplay between having something one wants to express, and being motivated to master the necessary skills to express it. However, this is only one aspect. More important is the fact that such work, with its personal involvement and inter-action between people, develops thought and reflection, leads to a deepening and refining of emotion, the cultivation of the senses, and the development of imaginative insights. In short, such work helps the child to grow towards maturity.

Sometimes the child will make recognizable to us as outsiders the personal significance of an experience. It is always difficult, however, to evaluate such qualities as sincerity, originality, feeling, and imagination in children's work. One tends to tire of collections of writing by unknown children, which is interpreted by compilers in their own way and set before us as models of what children can do if taught properly. Moreover, this sort of evaluation of children's work in terms of artistic value is often as alien to the more important aspects of teaching as 'English exercises' aimed at a certain kind of efficiency. What are important are the intellectual and sensory processes the child goes through as he reaches the point of expression, and the feelings of the shared experience. Sometimes the finished product may only hint at some of the long term objectives; sometimes it may reveal nothing of them. The teacher must not twist the result or impose his own interpretation on it for his own satisfaction. Instead, during the shared experience, the teacher will pick up sufficient nuances and clues to confirm him in his belief that these long term objectives are gradually being realized. This will enable him to avoid the error of assuming, in the absence of what he considers a 'good' piece of work, that nothing has happened to the child. Equally, although the teacher will always strive for a product that represents the child's best he must sometimes have a purpose and look for a result beyond the child's immediate artefact.

The role of the teacher

The role of the teacher can be defined fairly easily in thematic work, and it is a much more positive role than in other forms of teaching. It gives the teacher authority without the dressage or impedimenta that authority has assumed previously. It is the teacher's function to direct and channel the work so that the ways to and from the thematic area will be varied but co-ordinated. He is the person who should spark off the experience, although he can do nothing unless the child becomes involved of his own accord. It is he who should open the door to awareness for the children, and they in turn will look to him with a sense of trust as they progress in their own exploration of the theme. They may turn to him as much from the realization of failure to achieve an aim as from a wish to share a success. Although the children will frequently be the initiators, and the teacher will learn from their insights, there can be no abdication of his responsibilities. The function of the teacher is to teach, with all that is implied by that magical word. By this I do not mean that the teacher necessarily has to instruct the children in certain fields, or direct them into attitudes, conventions, or styles. However, he must ensure that the children have the widest possible range of experience from which to gain insight, sympathy, and understanding, for unless he sets out positively to do this, they will remain captives of their own immaturity and environment. Children are held on a very loose rein which can, if necessary, be used to redirect them to a path the teacher

considers will be advantageous to them. I am sure that everyone has seen
enough of the sloppy, purposeless, time-wasting activities sheltering under
the umbrellas of 'self-expression', 'free-expression', and 'discovery' to
realize that this must be so.

Here I must express my doubts about the extension of thematic work
into such fields as social studies, which often occurs when a project or
topic approach is used. In many of the themes presented later in this book
there is ample opportunity for other work of great value if the purpose and
possibilities of a subject are thoroughly explored, and if the teacher does
not hesitate to guide the activity as he thinks fit. But the use of investigation or research must be demanded by the purpose of the theme, for
otherwise the theme will easily develop into a very facile search for factual
knowledge which really involves the interest of very few children. I suspect
there is more time wasted on 'topic work' in junior schools than on anything
else. The motivation is lacking, the methods often amount to little more
than random copying from a book, and the topic becomes an obstacle to
that full imaginative involvement so necessary for learning. I am strongly
in favour of extending these themes into other fields of work, as long as
the teacher plays a full part in making the children aware of the different
possibilities for development and does not leave them to 'Find out all you
can about . . .' or 'Choose a topic of your own about . . .' To be fair, I fully
realize that this is overstated. Any method, after all, is as good as the teacher
who practises it.

Themes provide a framework for the teacher and the child. Although I
am arguing for width of experience, there is no contradiction in empha-
sizing the necessity of the limits that are imposed by such a framework.
Within this framework, the teacher has to isolate aspects of the subject on
which the children can concentrate, in order to make it possible for them
to order their feelings and ideas. One of the teacher's many tasks is to
break down the areas of the subject in order to give an opportunity for
their full exploration. It is only through this continual narrowing of the
field that the children can eventually become involved in a meaningful
experience of the whole thematic area. Examples of this isolation of aspects
of the subject are common in the themes in Part II. Thus the teacher can
hope to create a heightened awareness of one particular aspect of the
theme, which can then be extended to embrace a wider area. For example,
a child is not asked simply to write about a person, but rather teacher and
child together isolate elements of that person. The child explores stance,
gesture, small body movements, intonation, speech pattern, and so on, in
a variety of ways, and from each of these explorations the teacher tries to

develop an increased sensitivity, both to the details, and the whole, of the person. Only by this method will we really get creative work, because it will be the fruits of a detailed observation and feeling. Children cannot create in a vacuum nor in a field so wide as to confuse the issue and blur the edges.

As an example, let us take the theme **Animals**. Most teachers are aware of the special rapport between children and animals and know that children can be prompted to write about animals without a great deal of stimulation. Such writing often seems to be woolly, because it has not been channelled to make the most of children's observation and the sensory awareness they have of animals. The feelings aroused in children when first meeting young animals, for example, are strong, but undefined and amorphous. Ben in *A Dog so Small* (Philippa Pearce), Drem in *Warrior Scarlet* (Rosemary Sutcliff), and Karana in *Island of the Blue Dolphins* (Scott O'Dell) all demonstrate how, in different situations, similar feelings are evoked and expressed by the authors. Through talking and writing, through drama and art, this feeling can be crystallized, and the universal 'Aahh . . .' with which young animals are greeted will come to have a meaning and significance for children. So the teacher can deal with the more specific physical aspects of animals—the hamster's cold paws, the dog's nose, the particular look in an animal's eyes—or concentrate upon such emotions as protection, care, dependence, comfort, or revulsion. The scope is very wide, but the quality of children's creative work will only be high when the feelings are separated and the child is encouraged to focus on a particular aspect of a subject.

It is in this highlighting of a small aspect of the subject that the skill and authority of the teacher in thematic work is most evident. The teacher must decide which part of the whole is to be considered by the children for a particular time and direct his 'input' to this aspect. The responsibility of the teacher is awesome, for he will not only have to break the theme up into elements, but will then have to structure his material around those elements as they fit together in the whole theme. It is a process of detailed focusing on a single aspect; and then of feeding in all the teacher is able to, so that the child will have basis for his thoughts, attitudes, and expression. Later the theme will be brought together again and seen as a total of its parts; but unless we deal with the parts first, there can be no total other than a generalized impression that can have very little impact on the child.

Sharing experiences

The question of personal emotions in schools has undergone something of a change in the past few years. I do not think that students now are exhorted, as I was, not to become emotionally involved with their children. It is increasingly recognized that the emotional make-up of people, both children and adults, and the need to come to terms with feeling if personality is to develop fruitfully, are important. Teachers are no longer afraid of emotion in the classroom, or the expression of such emotion. Willingness to share emotion is essential to any form of artistic creation. Nor do teachers have to think that their attempts to extend insight and deepen understanding are beyond their younger children. (The 9 year old child is not a baby, though perhaps he will assume a baby's bib so long as he is fed baby food.) If one of the teacher's purposes is to help children think and feel, then emotions must first be awakened and afterwards shared and realized through the situation that the teacher develops with the children. I am not asking that teacher and children should share in an emotional orgy, nor am I forgetting the claims of children under special duress. What I am pleading for is a re-appraisal of the teaching situation that applies in particular to what might be termed the artistic experiences. There has been a proper decline in the position of the absolute authority of the teacher. This has had the effect of increasing the responsibility of the teacher, and calling forth qualities other than those needed in more authoritarian days.

Two aspects of sharing must particularly be considered: that between children, and that between teacher and child. The former is not difficult to achieve. It means that children are given every chance to discuss amongst themselves what they are doing, to see and listen to each other at work, to criticize and evaluate each other's achievements. Then, as a climax, maybe they can join in some communal presentation of work—say, in an exhibition, or a display. However, I think it is the sharing between teacher and child that gives our work a new dimension. In these themes the teacher explores many facets of experience with the children. Just as he realizes that some aspects of the theme will become special to the child, so the child should realize that some aspects are special to the teacher. He is not perhaps so much teaching the children as learning with them and this, then, becomes the essence of sharing. We as teachers must lead the children to see that some things matter to us, and let them share in our joys and excitements so that we fully use our personality as we teach.

Organizing a theme
The first thing, of course, is to pick a theme. The range of subjects seems unlimited and so the chief difficulty is that of choice. Ideally the choice of

theme should come from the children. In practice I have always found this difficult. I think the only way is for the teacher to choose the theme from his knowledge of the children. Themes can be introduced in many ways: **Cowboys and Indians** arising from a discussion of T.V. programmes; **Circuses and Fairs** from listening to Belgian café piano music; **Storms** from news of trawlermen in difficulties, and so on. The teacher should know what he wants, to start and structure the situation so that this comes about. This may seem Machiavellian, but in view of the range of material needed, and the careful selection and organization involved, I am convinced it is inevitable. Even where the initial interest arises from topics introduced by the children themselves, the choice of what to pursue and develop further is the teacher's. It is from his range of reading and experience that he provides the materials and situations which make the thematic development possible.

As the confidence of the teacher grows, themes begin to develop even to the extent of overlapping. A **Storm** theme becomes concerned with giants through the reading of James Reeves' 'Giant Thunder' (see p. 91), and much time was spent on developing this; **Cowboys and Indians** became **Animals**; and so on. In the early experience of this work teachers often say 'If only I had more time I would take that up ...' with a feeling that once a theme is started it has to be continued. Later the opportunities will be seized by those sensitive enough to spot them. Certainly it is a question of confidence. The most difficult step is probably the first; once this is taken, the work acquires a momentum of its own. With juniors I have never found any problem once the work is begun, but colleagues tell me it can be very different with older children.

It is important to remember, when choosing and planning a theme, that the point, or wholeness, of the work has to be clear to the child. The great danger of applying an adult concept of the unity of a theme must be avoided. Recently I saw a very gifted teacher plan a theme on **Spring**, seeing it clearly in terms of re-awakening of nature, of work, of emotion, and so on. Although she hoped to bring these together and lead the children to realize their unity, she was clever enough to admit her failure, for her planning was, in fact, too sophisticated for her young children. They could not see the point of the work as a whole and lost their zest for what seemed isolated fragments. The children must know what they are doing as clearly as the teacher does.

So, presuming a theme which has a flexible but fairly clear purpose has been chosen, a feeling of involvement has been generated, and a range of activity has been produced which will interest as many children as possible, what is the next step? Obviously there cannot be a set pattern; indeed there must not be. The development of a theme is a very personal matter, which no two people will approach in the same way. Much of what I have said so far emphasizes the validity of the teacher's personal preferences. Although, for the purposes of this book, I have kept to an arrangement of reading, drama, and writing in the themes which follow, this is not intended as a rigid schedule. I have often begun with reading, but this is only because it is my own preference. Ideally, the material should be handled flexibly, with different starting points being used. In the interaction of a variety of disciplines each is equally important; literature and drama are certainly not included simply to serve written expression. They have a value of their own separate from any other activity. (The reader may care to look at the section on p.21 on the difficulty of assessing dramatic involvement and quality.) The permutations are wide: writing followed by drama and literature; reading, moving into drama, and then splitting the class into two parts (reversed next time) one to do art and the other writing. In this case, the effect of the two groups upon each other can be quite remarkable. Or perhaps we begin with drama, followed by writing, then back to drama again with the children being asked to evaluate the effect of one upon the other. So we can ring the changes. Each teacher must decide for himself the order best suited to his purpose and working conditions.

We must remember that, as the theme continues, there will be 'drop outs', children who are pursuing a particular line of work and who must be allowed to finish it. It is very important to allow the child time and freedom to continue the work uninterrupted, even if it means the reading of a book or the making of a picture all afternoon.

To summarize, there are three vital steps in thematic work:
a. The planning of the theme. (This is best demonstrated by a 'flow diagram').
b. The collection of source material.
c. The 'internal planning' to organize rooms, other teachers, T.V. and radio, visits, visitors, and all the minutiae that are so important.

Some elements of a theme

Literature and reading

The tradition of telling stories and reading to children is well established in primary schools. It is always a great joy to see teachers animating the words of a story, part reading, part acting, part telling, and constantly inviting participation so that all the time something is happening to make the story live. In junior classes it is common practice for a story to be read straight through in serial form by the teacher. Obviously there is nothing wrong with this but I think it underestimates the potential of books and stories. Literature is at the heart of English teaching, since it is the primary means of enriching experience and of giving opportunities for active involvement, and provides an extension, or even a model, of linguistic imagery.

In the last few years there has been a great growth in books aimed at developing children's writing and reading by selections from poetry and literature. Many of these anthologies are extremely good, but in thematic work we are concerned with more than the specific skills of reading and writing. Words, passages, poems must be selected from all that is available in order to illuminate an aspect of our theme, and thereby start the children on the path of personal development. Some of these extracts will be short, their value lying in their fresh viewpoint, and their function as a source of discussion, but they should be read continually, at any time of every day, as a means of nourishing the children. The teacher should read many things— complete stories, extracts related to themes, snippets he has chanced upon —but the choice must always be very carefully considered, for much of the success of the work will depend upon the readings. (A useful book in this area is *Only Connect*, an anthology compiled by L. F. Ashley, *et. al.*)

Unfortunately, choice is not easy as it depends on our knowledge of children and children's books. When new books come along at today's rate, it is easy to see why teachers fall back on what they liked when young in determining what to read aloud. So much that is excellent in contemporary writing for children can pass us by. It is a fact that teachers' knowledge of current children's fiction is minimal. It might almost seem that, since schools are concerned with learning, teachers have considered it their duty to keep abreast with non-fiction in order to supply a book on 'castles', for example, at will, but that fiction is considered to be outside the field of essential knowledge. There is little hope for the improvement of this position unless teachers simply read more themselves. There are publications, reviews, and displays available, all of which help to sort out children's literature, but sooner or later teachers have to read what people put out for children in order to assess its worth. I find that once teachers take up this work, both reading children's fiction and talking about it amongst themselves, they find great personal pleasure in it. For it is true to say that a children's book which does not appeal to an adult is not a good children's book. I would not read anything to children that I had not genuinely appreciated myself. I think one must beware of accepting as good what one thinks children ought to like (a trap into which reviewers often fall). However, one must also be sure that stories do not demand a background of experience that is beyond the children. This is not to plead for simplicity but rather for selection and relevance. The time may come, and I believe is coming, when colleges of education do more about children's fiction, for, while it is a fine discipline for students to study literary giants of the past, people like Leon Garfield, Alan Garner, and Rosemary Sutcliff could offer equally fruitful fields of study for future teachers.

What, then, are we to do with literature? Undoubtedly there is a place for reading a whole story in instalments and I would not decry this (I still remember clearly stories read to me in this way). The trouble is that it is not sufficient, and if we consider our purposes I think we can see why. When the teacher reads with children he is trying to get them to see that literature is concerned with their own lives, both real and imaginary. They are looking at a common experience, an aspect of which is being highlighted through someone else's eyes; seeing how a particular writer orders the experiences; and being invited to join in. This is the whole purpose of my selections of readings in individual themes. Before a child does anything on **Storms**, for example, of which his direct experience will be limited, he hears about a variety of storms affecting a variety of people—children, seamen, climbers, animals, refugees, travellers—all described from different viewpoints. So the teacher needs to read a great number of passages to the children, often at odd spare moments, so that ideas in them can be discussed and allowed to ferment. Teachers should read to children every day of the week, even when the children are proficient readers themselves. These short sessions can go on in between readings from another complete story. I have found this method to have two great advantages. First, it leads children to read for themselves: when the teacher reads an extract and leaves the book available, it is immediately taken by a child and a queue forms for it. One of our main tasks as teachers is simply getting children to want to read books, so that they can themselves enjoy the private world of the book. Nowadays paperbacks are the great source of reading material, and this is my reason for picking many in the readings listed. The children should be led to buy or borrow these books after hearing the extracts, thus developing both the quality and quantity of their reading of fiction. I think that in the early teens, say from the age of 10 onwards, there is a grave decline in reading by children. There may well be many reasons for this, but in view of the great efforts made to teach them to read, it seems a great pity.

It is also necessary to consider the organization of the readings which the teacher has selected. These will be arranged to suit the aspect of the theme which is to be considered; but most important of all is the choice of the actual material to be read. The problem of the poor reader is always with us, and there is the additional problem of the difficulty of some of the passages. It is a fact that if the teacher is searching to extend insight and the appreciation of feelings, then there are not a great many examples in fiction for younger children, so he has to select judiciously and use commonsense. Some material I would hesitate to put directly before certain older pupils, but would willingly read parts to quite young children. The fact that children cannot read a book does not mean that they should not hear it, and discuss points appropriate to age and intelligence. This is an essential means of giving children extended models of language. So the teacher will often read his chosen extracts to the children, rather than the children reading for themselves. Sometimes both teacher and children will read, provided that the children are allowed to practise reading first, or perhaps to record their reading. Many of the poems and extracts are quite short and can be written on card for display to the children, or duplicated for their folders.

An example may help, so let us consider the theme **Fights**. It was decided to work under six headings, each of which would take about five hours a week, with perhaps a last week spent on bringing everything together. The headings chosen were Wrestling, Children Fighting, Gang Fights, Fist Fights, Fencing, and Animal Fights. The readings were grouped under these headings and each section had its own movement/drama, art, and writing developments, often interwoven, from which the children were able to make choices as the theme progressed. The wrestling section, for example, began with the reading from the wrestling scene in *A Kid for Two Farthings* (W. Mankowitz), and the poems 'Wrestling' (J.C. Ranson, in Harraps' *Junior Book of Modern Verse*) and 'All-in Wrestlers' (James Kirkup, in *Voices* 3). The movement began with strong and light movements, and later, accompanied by children's own sounds, combined in a pattern of contrasting movements. This was then continued in the art work with the children experimenting by making strong and light patterns in colour in a variety of media, accompanied by their own sounds, and in writing using strong and light words. This strong and light experience obviously carried over into other parts of the work and the awareness of movement pattern became a marked feature of the work. Here are two very individual views of a wrestling match, that were written during work on this theme.

> The dark black silhouettes
> Near the wall where the
> melting gold cinders burn
> on the fire.

My eyes are fixed as though
watching a skeleton
on a string,
The twisting of the arms
I long to see
But all I see is shadows
Twining together like branches
of big black trees.
All is quiet as
the smoke like mist settles
on my hat,
The fight has ended as though someone
had left me alone.
                    HEATHER BUTLER (*aged 10*)

His body bulged with strength
Might courageous
Blood
Trickled down my face.
He groaned
My waist creaked with pain.
His body twisted
and turned with mine.
He growled with rage.
He pulled,
My body was slowly
very slowly
turned to the ground
His face was going redder than red
His
Snake-like grip
clung to my shoulders
With one painful crunch
My shoulders touched the ground.
He had won.
                    TAMRYN PENROSE (*aged 10*)

The roles of the spectators, referee, photographers, seconds, and slow-motion cameramen all came to be included in the movement experience. At one time in movement the fist became the centre of pattern making. The children later made some fascinating models of fists in clay, and wrote like this:

Fists

Look at a person's hand
        Gentle
            Kind,
                Some beautiful.

But look at a clenched hand
 Cold
   Cruel,
     Angry.
Hands are different the way you hold them.
Look at the hand of a doctor
    The hand of a boxer
What a difference.
The doctor willing to help
The boxer willing to fight
   or
   Even kill
A boxer makes more work for a doctor than a
car does.

     MARGARET BREARLY (*aged 10*)

Fists open, Kind and gentle
Fists closed
Hard, Harsh and hateful
Fists shut, nobbly and round
Fists open
Wrinkled but soft.
Fists tight, tendons
Show through,
Fists open
So thoughtful, so kind.
The fist of man should not be closed.
    It gives him the feeling of hate.

    RAYMOND POWERS (*aged 10*)

Later the dramatic possibilities of wrestling were explored, with all the work ending in a class drama of wrestling. The children finished their efforts and entered into another theme.

Speech

In recent years research into the whole field of linguistics has developed considerably. This research, particularly into children's language development, has offered teachers very important insights. I can only refer in this section to those points which seem to me most significant, but in the Bibliography (p.175) there is a selection of books for the teacher who may wish to go further.

The word 'speech' means different things to different people. In *Growth through English,* (O.U.P. for N.A.T.E., 1967) John Dixon points to some of the ambiguities implicit in the word, and to the relationship of speech to writing and drama. Talking is such a part of our lives that we should not need to consider it at all. It is a person's primary means of communication; it is how we sort ourselves out, classify our impressions, and live our lives, both real and fantastic. Yet we know that, while the language environment of a growing child is probably the most important factor in the development of both oracy and literacy, many children have limited opportunities for a satisfactory adult/child dialogue in their homes. This dialogue is fundamental to their linguistic growth. Additionally we seem to have built up barriers against talk in our schools, perhaps as a legacy of our Victorian heritage, where 'to be seen and not heard' was a prime virtue in children, or perhaps as a result of our very large classes. It is easy to understand the difficulty of giving adequate opportunity for speech in a class of forty children, and yet we know that spoken language is developed only by speaking, just as written language is learned by writing. It is as simple and yet as difficult as that; all language is learned by use in response to a situation that calls for it, and not in isolated English periods concerned with rules or structures divorced from the child's own involvement. The difference in the willingness to use and experiment in spoken language between the infant in his first years at school and the junior who is leaving is depressing. The atmosphere must still often be wrong. Both play and conversation are regarded as 'not work' and hence have no place in classrooms. I think one further reason for the teacher's neglect of oracy may well lie in his own feelings of insecurity. The written work that children do leaves a record of a teacher's influence and industry. Someone might notice it, or at least it can be produced on Open Days, and when the county inspector calls, whereas talking just leaves us exhausted, with no obvious evidence of achievement.

In the themes which follow I have included instructions such as 'Talk it over first', 'Tell someone what you are trying to do', 'Discuss this with each other' in many places. These phrases are included because I am sure it is vital that every opportunity for the practice of talking is taken. It is certainly no easy task to get children to talk purposefully if they are unaccustomed to it, but the idea does catch on, and even the teacher who starts in unfavourable circumstances will make progress if he sets out to create the right conditions of confidence and honesty. The teacher must ensure that children have something to talk about and then take his special place in the sharing process that talking implies, extending the modes of language wherever he can, and remembering, above all, that we are concerned more with 'appropriateness' in speech than a pre-conceived idea of 'correctness'. Hence the temptation to correct speech should be largely resisted. It will be obvious that in an atmosphere such as this, the 'oral English' exercise so beloved in course books will have no part to play.

Children talking and writing

The difference between writing and talking, and the interaction of the two, is worth consideration. Whereas the young child will write as he speaks (in fact his earliest writing experience is of the teacher writing down what he says), the older child will not. He comes to realize that there are different conventions to be obeyed. In terms of fluency it is, oddly enough, speech that usually suffers. Perhaps this is because the child, in some school situations, loses confidence in the value of talk. Even where talk is fostered, he may become inhibited and self-conscious in the immediacy and directness of spoken exchanges. He comes to appreciate the privacy of writing (particularly if the teacher is not always looking over his shoulder), and the opportunity it allows for alteration and modification. The advantage of writing is that it is a reflective activity, leaving time for reconsideration, for the evaluation of words, and for the re-calling and re-forming of experience. Through both speech and writing we seek to translate experience into the manageable reality of words, and indeed, in some respects, until we have found the words we haven't had the experience. In certain situations children need the privacy and reflective opportunities of writing, in others the rapid interchange, the improvisation, personal stimulus, and response that talk provides. While I am sure that all writing should be preceded by talking, and, somewhere along the line, writing is refined through talking, it would be a mistake to expect too great a correlation between the two forms. Children will frequently, and at different times, be more fluent in one form than the other. Equally we should never regard talking just as the handmaiden of writing. As a skill alone speech will be more necessary than writing for many children. It is somewhat ironic that, while we all know the 9 or 10 year old who is an interesting, willing conversationalist but who can scarcely read and who writes abominably, we spend far more time on what is virtually a hopeless battle to achieve the writing and reading skills he will hardly need than we do on developing this necessary skill in speech.

Writing

So much has been said and written lately about children's creative writing that there has emerged something of a bandwagon loaded with educationalists instructing children on how and what to create. I think we delude ourselves if we ignore the regrettable fact that the fund of real creativity is spread very thinly over mankind in general, and inevitably not much of it will touch many children. Although we are concerned with immersing children in experiences from which they will gain an understanding that can be expressed, all children do not react to an experience with the same depth of feeling, and they vary in their ability to express it. This is an argument in favour of width of experience, so that as many children as possible may have access to a personal experience which will stimulate them into expression of some kind. It is not an admission that attempts by children to be creative are largely doomed to failure, but a plea for a better understanding of the terms we use. Many teachers become confused about their aims when they hear terms like 'free expression', 'creative writing', 'personal writing', 'imaginative writing', bandied about, and leaving them in the end to make up their own minds about the meaning of such words and the value of such work. How, for example, should the Newsom Report's phrase 'free outpourings' be interpreted? In *The Use of English*, Vol. 19, No.4, Michael Alcott quotes some of these phrases from a number of respected and important sources 'not for the purpose of ridicule or attack but to point out that English teachers are working with an ill-designed concept for a vague aim!'

We must not lose the ground we have gained in the field in recent years, but these aims must be defined if our achievements are to be fruitful. Far too much ill-disciplined, personally dishonest, prettiness passes as creativity. This would be forgiveable, if it were not also praised! I know a child who writes very well. When she showed me a piece of writing, a poem on autumn, I asked her why she had done it; the reply was 'Miss X told me to!'. Was she being creative or was she laughing at me and keeping Miss X happy and quiet? Or there is the story of the 12 year old girl whose teacher told me she was good at English, but didn't do as she was told. When I questioned this, the teacher quoted a time when she had taken a lesson on protest, and after readings, including extracts from writings of Ghandi and Martin Luther King, she had told the children to write something on protest. This child had gone away and written a piece about the rain on the windows!

I think, in fact, we are mostly concerned with *re-creation*. Our function, as teachers, is to enlarge the children's experience so that they can re-create from it. At its lowest level it means that we hare giving them a base, the desire to make something and the equipment that facilitates this. Often re-creation becomes a form of copying, which is not to be scorned, since one child can be using another's creation to make something for himself and of himself. This borrowing is something that probably all writers do at some time or another. (In *Teaching Poetry* James Reeves says of writing: 'Most immature poetry is written in imitation, direct or remote, of some poem which has appealed to the writer.') The child can, in relating to one attitude or point of view, accept it or reject it, and in so doing make something of it his own. In this act he must at some stage have a personal involvement with it. The piece of work which results will not all be his, but somewhere, sometime, there will be a personal and original view. In the poem by Heather Butler quoted earlier, the last line made it hers; the rest I suspect was an amalgamation of the teacher's and the poet's ideas and phrases, and the dramatic situations she had explored.

I am also often intrigued by the phrase 'imaginative writing'. What does this mean? Many teachers take it to mean putting children into an imaginary situation, usually of a highly coloured nature, and asking them to write about it. 'Imagine you are a cabin boy on a pirate ship. Tell what it is like.' This might well produce a good result but only if the background is explored discussed, animated, and, better still, if it is part of a theme 'Pirates', which would provide a full involvement in the relevant situations and experiences. Here two levels are involved—the situation and the language. We are seeking an explorative use of language in an unusual situation, one which the children may not have directly experienced but must imagine.

Children can be put in an imaginary situation through the use of a wide range of starting points. I have seen teachers working successfully with very varied physical or emotional stimuli—music, pictures, water, driftwood, textured materials, leaves, bark, and so on—upon which the children bring their sensory perceptions to bear and transcribe the feelings into an imaginary situation through language. Thus they can realize the situation as fully as possible. In passing I think the least desirable stimulus is to say to the children 'Imagine you are . . .'. On principle, I never use this phrase. Children do not 'imagine' themselves to be on a boat; they *are* on that boat and the situations we create through drama, literature, or music put them there. Things which children may never experience in reality can be made real to them in their imaginations, providing that we bear two things in mind. First that all imagination depends on the ability to create images, and secondly that this ability depends finally upon previous real experience. Although this division is an over-simplification, the distinction between six forms of imagery in Peter McKellar's *Imagination and Thinking* does help one realize that one's own kind of imagery may vary greatly from someone else's. So teachers need to use many different situations, and involve all the senses, if they are to harness the power of imagination in all their children.

At one time, in the attempt to make writing activities more relevant to children, they were asked to write about experience that was almost entirely concrete and direct. So they wrote about what they did, what they saw, how they did things, and the result was the proliferation of diary and news writing.

Some of this did use language creatively, but much of the writing was dull, repetitive, and constrained. I see no difference between functional and imaginative writing, although some people see one as clear and precise and the other as extravagant and rose-red! But the difference is only that of situation and how it is interpreted. In a sense a child uses all language imaginatively as he works to sort out his experience, either of reality or fantasy, and match it with words. This writing involves him in choosing and adapting from his store of language that which will best make his experience real and communicable.

Sense training

The place of sense training in children's creative work is very important. Ask a child to tell you about a familiar thing such as a toy, or his classroom, and you will be surprised at the poverty of the result. This may be due to an inadequate vocabulary but more likely it is due to a lack of sensory awareness.

The tactile sense is one teachers neglect dreadfully and yet they know how younger children like to touch, stroke, or nestle against different textures. I have mentioned earlier the importance of focusing on small aspects of a subject, and of detailed observation. A heightened sensory awareness can only be achieved if the field is narrowed and the child is asked to concentrate on one aspect of what he sees, hears, touches, or smells. We should try as far as we can to isolate each sense in such work. Thus a teacher may say to the children: 'Close your eyes while you feel this, now feel the floor; is there a difference?' Or 'listen to all the sounds in the room; how many can you hear? Try to pick out just one sound and listen to that. Can you hear yourself breathing? Can you hear the silence? Or 'Do you notice the difference in smell when you come into this room, or when you go into the caretaker's room, or into the cellar? Go and find out.' Examples of this sort of work are found in several of the themes developed later.

Children writing poetry

In recent years there has been a remarkable growth in the writing of poetry by children—a growth in quality as well as quantity. Most of this has been in what is usually called 'free verse'. The phrase is somewhat emotive and difficult to define. In fact there is no accepted definition, but what is usually meant is a form of writing that is free from the traditional structures of rhyme and metre, that enables language to be used creatively to express shades of thought and feeling in a rhythmic way. The reader should look at James Reeves, *An Anthology of Free Verse* for a further discussion of this subject.

The writing of poetry demands an imaginative effort and a fierce struggle with language at whatever level it is done. Poetry cannot be something we 'knock off' in a few minutes without any involvement. Unless teachers are prepared to help with the struggle and create situations where a personal surrender through imagination is possible, they are far better off to leave the attempt, and continue with stories and compositions. In *Trends in Education* (No. 12, October, 1968) Leonard Clarke has some interesting, and not always complimentary, things to say about the growing fashion of writing poetry. While I would not agree with him entirely, the danger of failure is too great for the attempt to be made lightly. However, the rewards of writing poetry are also great, and, unless we take the chance of showing children that writing poetry is the exercise of intellectual and imaginative powers, we do run the risk of educating another generation of adults in the same mould as ourselves. For the great majority of today's adults have no feeling for poetry whatsoever, and even see the writing or reading of it as a waste of time, although most of the same group would like some form of music, and some form of visual art.

There are two questions to answer. First, why do we encourage children to write poetry at all? And second, how do we get them to write the sort of poetry that will serve to promote their education? There are probably as many answers to these questions as there are committed teachers. In many ways the asking of questions like this is a more important exercise than answering them. The imagery of poetry, and the discipline of its form, make it different from children's other writing. In poetry, more than any other form of expression, every word matters, and the child has to be led to consider the worth of each word in expressing his thoughts and feelings. Clearly the teaching of poetry writing also has to be considered carefully. In the early years children will scarcely know they are writing poetry. The work might never be described to them in these terms. They are experimenting with form, striving to make each word contribute, and searching for images —all to express what they want to as clearly as possible. As they write like this, they will come to realize that some things can be said better in a poetic form, or indeed that some things can only be said in this way. Because of the freedoms from the normal constraints of prose, and of the subtlety of imagery, they may be able to express thoughts and feelings better in a poem. Among other things, a poet expresses common feeling and emotion in a way individual to himself. Through searching their own feelings thoroughly the children will become aware of common experience.

One means of developing a child's ability to express himself in poetic form is simply to surround the child with poetry of all kinds so that he can turn to it, whatever the situation, and see its relevance. The average adult has perhaps not met enough poetry, being confined to a rather restricted anthology, or to a teacher's choice, in his schooldays. In the past, too, the teaching of poetry was very concerned with 'meaning'. Younger children cannot be expected to 'understand' a poem in an adult sense of the word, but they can feel it, recognize some part of it in a sensitive way, and identify with it. From this point of view I think there is very little that is 'too difficult' for children, for this is the attitude that condemns young ones to a diet of daffy-down-dillies and bunnies in woolly caps! Our criteria must be that the poems the teacher selects for special attention in his work must be good in his judgement, and that they will give the child the chance for identification. In the following themes, I have tried to select poems which fit these criteria, and have listed what I consider to be good material within particular contexts.

The Plowden Report says, 'Some good teachers lack conviction about the value of poetry and are more confident about giving children opportunities to write poems than about nourishing them with great poetry.' This smacks of teaching a child to read without ever letting him see or hear a story. Perhaps the word 'great' is the stumbling block, since many still feel that a poem should be firmly established by critics in order to be acknowledged. Since we as teachers use poetry to illustrate life and to lead children to explore new worlds of thought and imagination, its relevance to these purposes is surely more important than some hypothetical 'greatness'. This is where modern poets have such an impact on children. Their force and economy can be like a cold shower in bringing them to a sharp awareness of their immediate surroundings. For these reasons I have included a number in the readings.

The writing of free verse has many advantages for children, but, if a child chooses to write in it, this should only mean that he finds the form most fitting for what he wants to say and the feelings he wishes to evoke. Whenever children write they should be free to select their own forms. Some will choose to write in free verse, some in rhyme, and others in prose. The possibility of choice is a necessary part of the development of each child. Until all forms of writing have been tried, a child's awareness of possibilities, a vital factor in his language development, will be restricted. One of the teacher's primary functions is to show him these possibilities and then allow time for experimentation with them.

Techniques of writing

Although I now have an almost pathological dislike, even hatred, of English exercises, I recognize the need for a purposeful practice to accompany or precede written work. Such practice cannot, however, be found in books. Teachers mostly realize this and yet they still buy, and even use, such books. I have yet to meet a teacher who thinks that working through English exercises produces any improvement in real terms. Certainly their use is deplored in the authoritative writing on the development of children's language skills. Exercises might be some help if used selectively to illustrate and practise a particular point a teacher wants to make, but they are more often used to justify a teacher than to help the children. Teachers have to decide what practice their children need, and not leave the decision to someone miles away growing fat on his royalties. This may be a little unfair, and, in classes of the present size, many teachers use such books as 'child occupiers' while they deal with other urgent problems. This may often be the only possible solution, being the sort of compromise for which the English nation is famous, as long as teachers admit that in so doing their children are not learning much, and do their utmost to remedy it elsewhere. Yet, let there be no mistake, teachers who really want to will find ways of teaching their children skills and techniques without resource to such activities. They obviously work a great deal harder, have different goals, and fortunately get a different reward. Still, what are teachers to do?

1. Teachers have to decide their priorities and choose their methods accordingly. Let me take an example. Children may write freely and well in what is loosely called a creative, imaginative way, but the teacher feels they need more experience in exact descriptive writing. I would suggest he chooses a theme he thinks can suit this purpose. In one like **Work**, for example, children can be called upon to describe activities they see on visits to factories, farms, and so on, or describe *exactly* the functioning of a body/machine shape they build up themselves.

2. Time has to be spent on techniques of punctuation, number, gender, tense, and so on. The nature of writing is different from other forms of expression and demands more conventions. These conventions form the basis of our grammar, and if writing is to be appropriate to the child, it is better if rules are mastered as the child's developing skill calls for their use. The dangers, of course, are obvious: primarily that the acquisition of such grammatical skills is never an end in itself. They are good habits to be used and it is the using that matters.

   Ideally the teaching of these habits should be individual, but this is obviously impossible. The teacher has to try to group together children who are showing the need for a rule or skill at such a time as will not interfere with their flow of language. These groupings will never be rigid but will alter almost from week to week, in size and personnel. (The teacher may decide, for example, that all the children, save the few very bright and the few very dull, need practice in capital letters for proper names. In this case the group may be very large.) Grouping is essential if our teaching is to be at all efficient, but it demands the keeping of adequate records by both teacher and child. The reader may care to look at *Recording Children's Progress* by Joan Dean for a more detailed study of this but I feel that every teacher really has to devise a recording system that suits him, one which is simple enough not to become a drudge, and clear enough to indicate possible groupings from time to time. The question of who and what to teach must arise from the teacher's marking and his observations of the children at work. While there is general agreement as to what the hypothetical average child should know of grammar, this can never be established in curriculum form. In general the items will arise at different times with different children and it is the teacher's skill in spotting the optimum times which makes for success.

3. A lot of time has to be spent on what can only be described as 'vocabulary work' or 'word study'. These practices will take their place as the work progresses. Their consideration will have an important place in the teacher's planning of the development of the theme.

Drama

I find it very hard to divorce literature and drama. If we look on literature as being a shared experience between teacher and child, as the mirror of our feelings, situations, and experiences, and as being a way to a deeper involvement through awareness, then we can say the same about drama. It is also a vehicle for the development and expression of that awareness, which is as valuable as writing or art. The first question is probably 'Why do drama?'. Here the temptation to claim too much for drama must be resisted. The field itself is so ill-defined in schools that it is hard to know what we are evaluating, and I would be loath to claim its virtues for all that can pass as drama. Done badly it can range from the rigid, formalized, and teacher-controlled to the unorganized, superficial, and chaotic. At each of these extremes it is a travesty of artistic work. Drama can mean anything from infants performing a scripted nativity play to improvised dance. Therefore, at its best, what is drama, and what can it do? Opinions here can be conflicting, for a drama specialist will sometimes advance claims for his subject so complex as merely to confuse the practising teacher. Amongst other things he may see it as having a neurological value as a result of the mental, physical, and emotional qualities working in unison for the education of the 'whole' man. Many teachers, on the other hand, hold the view 'that drama in the primary schools is not a subject or discipline but rather a method of, or an aid to, teaching' (*Drama Education Survey* 2, H.M.S.O.) To me drama is another facet of exploration which leads to re-creation, with the great asset that it involves children physically as well as mentally and emotionally. Any physical exploration of language leads to drama. In any form, from infants dramatizing in their play upwards, it is part of the educative process involving an imitation which is the root of our early intuitive learning.

Perhaps it might be more relevant to consider why it is that so few teachers do any sort of drama at all. It may be that they are unable to see a worthwhile purpose in it and they flounder on the question of 'Where do we go now?' So the whole thing becomes a nebulous, almost recreational activity without a result. I could not imagine drama as a lesson on its own in primary or middle schools. It is part of the general teaching situation, and the elements of mime, movement, speech, music, and improvisation must be integrated with children's other activities.

Drama is a progressive activity. As situations of growing complexity arise, children will search for form and the selective powers to handle them. We know that in early years, children's drama goes on and on, and it is later that we want them to get experience of dramatic shape—the idea of climaxes, beginnings and endings, and so on. Similarly in movement, we want them gradually to reach a stage where movements are developed and combined into sequences. As in most aspects of creative work, I do not think that progression lies in altering the nature of the experience, but rather in changes in the quality of the response we expect from that experience. The same activity can be performed by the 5 year old as the 10 year old, except that the older child will show a higher degree of awareness and skill. In fact there is much to be said for deliberately setting the same activities and challenges for different ages, so that the child can bring his increased skills to bear on a familiar situation. The teacher should always bear in mind, however, the particular skill he is trying to foster. If the improvisations are designed for imaginative work, so all discussion should be concerned with this, and work on weaknesses of shape, movement, or speech should be deferred to another time, although this time should probably occur within the confines of the particular theme. Ultimately a balanced approach by the teacher will cater for both the specific quality to be fostered and the general weaknesses which need to be practised, but they cannot usually be dealt with at the same time.

Some practical points to bear in mind during dramatic work are listed below:

1. We are concerned with drama, not theatre. Theatre is concerned with relationships between an actor and an audience; drama is a purely personal struggle of the person within himself. In drama children come to realize themselves and express the shades of feeling which are relevant to themselves alone. While I would agree that drama is never a solitary, or even completely introspective, activity, I believe that the child's own expression through movement is the primary function of drama. While the child will be aware of, consider, and respond to others, it is in himself that the dramatic event really happens. Only he can know and assess that. Teachers will strive to increase the boundaries of relevance through increasing his awareness, but the secret lies with him alone.

Children's Song

We live in our own world,
A world that is too small
For you to stoop and enter
Even on hands and knees,
The adult subterfuge.
And though you probe and pry
With analytic eye,
And eavesdrop all our talk
With an amused look,
You cannot find the centre
Where we dance, where we play,
Where life is still asleep
Under the closed flower,
Under the smooth shell
Of eggs in the cupped nest
That mock the faded blue
Of your remoter heaven.

R.S. THOMAS (*Song at the Year's Turning*)

2. As is the case with writing, technique is used as a means of enriching expression, and is not for the benefit of the teacher but of the child. I think the two main techniques involved at this level are 'space aware-ness' and 'body parts'. Both of these must be taught. No worthwhile movement is possible until a child is able to use space properly and be fully aware of the parts of the body he is using. In early years a great deal of time has to be spent inducing the children to look about them, and to 'take their space' with them. The latter in particular involves being conscious of other people and leaving them room to work in,

moving around without crashing into others, and having a place in a crowded area where one can be alone. It is a skill that needs training and is the first essential in any movement work. If a teacher finds that children are deficient in this respect, he must go back and train them to look before expecting anything more. The use of body parts is not so obvious to children. In drama every part of the body matters and children do not naturally realize the capacity of each part to be expressive. The teacher continually has to call upon children to react with a specific part of the body—perhaps the hands, or eyes—or to let themselves be conscious of a reaction passing slowly through all parts of the body.

3. Initially children will overact or pantomime most situations. This is a necessary stage in development and they must be given opportunity to do so. Initial work on old people, for instance, will immediately generate a class full of decrepid, crippled humans. The time comes for the teacher to change this tendency by encouraging observation, concentration, and the focusing of attention upon one body part. It is impossible to say when this time arrives; the teacher must be sensitive to it and always be looking for opportunities to increase children's awareness. By directing attention to different parts of the body and the finer qualities of movement the teacher will overcome the tendency to overact, and achieve a truer picture of a situation. Some examples of this possible breakdown are given in the **People** theme.

4. Much is often made of the importance of imagination in children's dramatic work. I would not undervalue this, but the cornerstone of the work is concentration. A deeper intensity of concentration is needed in drama work than in most other things children are called upon to do. Its contribution to the development of concentration may in itself be one good reason for doing drama in schools. Certainly, I grow more and more convinced that through drama, concentration can be taught. Every lesson must begin with exercises designed to focus concentration and direct the attention inwards. As activities continue and, with younger children, change frequently, the teacher must watch carefully to ensure that the children are concentrating and, if he finds that they are not, return to exercises aimed at restoring concentration. The exercises are generally small and, as far as possible, involve the five senses. In some of the themes I have included these exercises, but they are not specific to any of the themes and can be applied elsewhere. Examples of exercises include listening to sounds, isolating them, listening to oneself, feeling different textures, making sounds of different kinds, re-assembling anything small or anything complex (a Dinky car, a

transistor set), examining and sorting imaginary objects, identifying shades of colour on a wall, watching shadows move, watching fish in a pond (and reaching in to catch one), building a dam to alter the pool, opening a safe, getting through an obstacle rigged with an alarm bell, working with a microscope, copying someone's writing, taking photographs of animals drinking at a water-hole, mounting insects or butterflies, or unravelling a ball of string.

5. Although we are not concerned with an audience and the entertainment of others is very low on our list of priorities, there is a great place for group and class work in the themes. Much of this is related to children's play activities, for we are trying to utilize and extend this play. I think there are certain principles to be kept in mind when developing a class drama.

   a. It must be child-centred. Basically it comes out of discussion with the children and it is this discussion which decides the form of finished work. One of the great values of class work is the preparation and team work it involves. As a member of this team a teacher may well have something in mind (e.g. an Indian attack, the Pied Piper story) and might have pointed the preliminary practices in that direction. I think this is fair teaching method and have never found children short of ideas once they have been given relevant experiences.

   b. The selection of roles must be left until the work is very well advanced. Every child must be given an opportunity to do every activity before a selection of individual roles is made.

   c. The final work must involve every child, although at different levels. Many children will find their own level of involvement directed by their personality, but everyone has a part to play.

   d. The normal progression from individual to group to class work can be varied with profit. The children could be asked to work as a group, then practise individually, then come back together as a group from time to time.

   e. Signals are important. The children must know when something is expected of them and what it is. For many teachers recorded music is the key here. If it is used, then the children must really have become familiar with it through frequent listening to the relevant passages. Alternatively, percussion can become the usual signal and the children come to respond to its sounds. In any case the use of percussion in drama is vital for its effect and stimulus, and, with a little practice, the teacher can learn to make a variety of sounds, as can children also, when working in groups.

f. I have met many teachers who have been afraid of drama, or at least
of trying to do some with children. It may be that some of the points
raised earlier account for this, but I suspect that in many cases it is
a question of class control. This is a pity because drama is easy and
anyone can do it. What is needed first of all is a specific *control*, a
signal at which children stop moving and be quiet instantly. This may
be a tap on a cymbal or a clap of the hands, but whatever it is children
have to have training in responding to it. This may take some time to
develop, but it must be insisted on if any real work is to come. The
teacher starting drama should make her control signal known from
the beginning and give children practice with it until she is quite sure
that she can gain an immediate response to it, no matter what is going
on. Chaos is not definable as an amount of noise, but as the time it
takes to stop the noise.

Speech and drama

An earlier section dealt with speech in the general classroom situation. Here
I will consider the role of talking in dramatic work. Sooner or later children
have to talk in drama. The great change in recent years has been the timing
of its introduction. Unfortunately, the meaning of language has been emphasized too much in the past. All speech has an intonation and tune which can
be interpreted apart from the meaning of the words. Initially language is
only sound, and this must be our first consideration. Children must have a
great deal of experience in making relevant sound before any sort of speech
can have a spontaneous quality.

1. Rhythm

From a very early age rhythm and emphasis are important aspects of language. Young children appreciate rhythm before meaning and seem to have a
natural feeling for it. In her recording of pre-sleep monologue of her two
year old son, Anthony, R.H. Weir shows him repeating syllables in a pattern-
ed way for no other apparent purpose than pleasure (*Language in the Crib*).
Stories with rhythmic, repetitive patterns are children's earliest literary
experience and continue to charm for many years. The reader will know
the importance of these patterns in nursery and folk tales and will have
noticed the rhythmic appeal of words. Wait for young children to join
in when things like Wanda Gág's *Millions of Cats*, or T.S. Eliot's 'Macavity the
Mystery Cat' (see p.115) are read and see then the way thay respond to
a pattern. Initially, a fairly simple phrase can be selected, either one created
by one of the children to suit a situation, or one selected from the readings
—for example, 'hag wife, hag wife, bring me my bones' **(Storms)**, 'Is there

anybody there?' (**Mysteries**), 'My mother said ...' (Skipping rhyme, **Children**). The children should be asked to practise saying a phrase in as many ways as they can before selecting one finally. To each of the ways they have practised they can then fit body movements. Finally, they can select one rhythm of speech and movement, and practise the two together until they become a firm pattern in their minds and are integrated into further actions. The important thing is to get children to listen to the sounds they make and eventually to differentiate between these sounds. With concentration they can hear the sounds in their heads without making any noise. Ask the children to pretend they are speaking through a hand-held microphone. When a signal (a tap on the head or a beat on the drum) is given, it means that the microphone has been taken away and the voice will be heard. Or simply ask them to close their eyes and say something over and over to themselves until they pick out the best way to say it; then let the signal come as an indication that it can now be said. These practices will also be concerned with sounds other than words—the noise of the wind, a creaking door. (Sounds in the 'wild wood' in **Mysteries** can be considered in this way.)

The refinements, for practised teachers, include getting children to work to other children's spoken rhythms, either in pairs or groups, and chorus work, involving both body and voice. I would like to tell of one fascinating piece of work I saw recently on the theme **Fire**. The children were asked to think of 'fire' words and sounds, and we got such phrases as 'flickering shadows', 'spitting logs', 'banging and crashing', 'leaping', 'smokey blue colours', together with some sounds. After practising these sounds and words the children were grouped closely together, told to shut their eyes and say their sounds or words when they were tapped on the head. At first the teacher did the tapping, then he was joined by others who created almost a symphony of spoken sound, playing on the children like a number of instruments, and incorporating climatic and background noises. The final effect was wonderful. I thought at the time that the degree of concentration brought by the children to this work was as great as anything I had seen for a long time.

2. From sound to speech
After practice with movement to sound, and with rhythmic patterns of sound, the next step is to move further towards language with meaning by using the form of speech commonly known as 'mumbo-jumbo' or 'gibberish'. Children like experimenting with words in an inventive way, and should be encouraged to do so. The language of Clive King's *Stig of the Dump*, or of the boys at play in Keith Waterhouse's *There is a Happy Land* suggests an opportunity to play with words in a delightful way. Children are asked to

talk in an invented foreign language using sound in the way words would be, but without the structure of exact language. At first the tasks given to them should be quite specific: to describe something they have made, to ask the way somewhere, to give instructions, to meet someone and introduce themselves, to be angry, to be nervous, to be sympathetic to a lost child, and so on. In each of these situations there is a quality to the language which the child must come to realize. (Many years ago the anthropologist Malinowski drew attention to this role of speech—not so much to convey the meaning in any intellectual sense, but to convey feeling.) A child will eventually develop the ability to express himself in some form through 'gibberish', and later to relate his own sound to someone else's. A dialogue will develop more fluently than in ordinary speech, because 'gibberish' calls for more response than the frequent 'You did', 'I didn't', which is occasioned only by lack of language. An argument might develop perhaps, a buyer and seller situation, a discussion about an imaginary object or something that has been done. Only when the children concentrate more on what they are expressing than on formal words, can they move on to use these words for expressing themselves in drama. But a great deal of work on rhythm and 'gibberish' will be necessary before speech can be used in movement/drama. When the speech is natural and spontaneous, let it come; but do not rush into this field. Time spent on earlier stages is much to be preferred, and will eventually bring a greater reward.

Organization

Team teaching

Team teaching has tremendous possibilities. Lately, in the newer secondary schools, there has been a reaction against specialist teaching which is carried on in separate departments. This does not mean, however, that the specialist has no part to play. It simply means that his special skills, knowledge, and interests are to be differently employed. He becomes part of a team, making his contributions where most appropriate to the particular theme. I am certain that if a team of specialist teachers set out to organize a theme and each contributed from his own specialization, the value of the work as a whole would be increased. All that is needed is the conviction that the breaking down of subject barriers is worthwhile, and the will to break them down on everyone's part. If these are present, then the question of organization arises. Esmor Jones and Anthony Adams discuss this problem in depth at the secondary level in *The World in Words*. (See also Anthony Adams, *Team Teaching and the Teaching of English*.)

In primary schools generally there is, and always has been, a strong anti-specialist feeling. The reasons for this are well founded but they should not hide the fact that most teachers have some special interests and abilities which will colour their work. There is a great danger that the 'jack of all trades' philosophy will condemn children to a diet of dull mediocrity, a situation where everything is fair but nothing great. Creativity cannot flourish in such a climate. These specializations can be provided by different teachers without the children losing the security and continuity they need, particularly at a young age.

One of the teacher's responsibilities in thematic teaching is to make children aware of the most relevant aspects of an experience, through personal involvement on both sides. Teachers should seek to make these highlights of experience available to children from as wide a range of sources as possible, so that as many children as possible will be personally involved with the material. The possibility of relying on several teachers rather than one will increase the range of experience through which involvement will occur.

If team teaching is to work, teachers cannot be imprisoned in the strait-jacket of prescribed ratios of teachers to children, and in particular the rigid idea of one teacher to one class. Just as some work needs a quiet atmosphere and some can go along happily in a noisy one, so some work can quite properly be taken with large groupings while other work needs small ones. I have never found that a detailed timetable is either desirable or workable in primary schools; so perhaps we are looking for 'co-operative' rather than 'team' teaching. In the former situation teachers call upon each other when they need help, or realize that someone else has a special part to play. All it needs is for teachers to talk to each other about what they are doing; then suggestions for readings, music, or art work will readily appear. The value of this sort of co-operation to students or young teachers will be obvious. Equally, it will be a great advantage if there is a continuity of this type of work throughout the school. But what is the teacher to do where the conditions are entirely unsatisfactory—where perhaps they are working in a strictly timetabled school, or in a school where English exercises of the 'a _____ of geese' ilk are held in high regard, or in a school where teachers regard the classes they teach and the ideas they use as 'my' children and 'my' ideas. Nor is it easy to have an expressive movement lesson when space is not readily available, when noise might distract other groups, or when a disapproving head tends to pop in at awkward moments. Even the most skilled and experienced teachers have these moments. I could not presume to provide solutions for all these situations.

These predicaments arise continually in many situations and demands are made upon us which are patently unfair. However, the teacher who is keen and committed will make thematic teaching work, in spite of the difficulties, because he is convinced that it is worthwhile. To say that difficulties should never prevent one from pursuing a course that one thinks is right is a platitude, but there is no other way to put it. Success in discouraging situations should influence others so that they too will wish to try, or at least to modify their usual methods.

Time allocation

The question of how much time should be spent on work based on themes is a hard one to answer. My impulse is simply to say 'a lot' but this is not much practical help. Yet the answer is relevant, for large blocks of time do need to be apportioned to this work. To start with, it cannot be done where the timetable is fragmented into short periods. Happily this is a declining state of affairs.

Much is heard these days of integration and, if this is practised in a school, there is no problem whatsoever. A theme simply becomes the area of work for as long as the teacher considers necessary. Where integration is not the teaching structure, I would say that three-quarters of the time usually spent on English, all of that usually spent on art, and all spent on movement should be grouped into *at least* three sessions (half days) in a week. If the theme is extended into history, geography, and so on, then times from these subjects can also be available. I do not think that this is asking for too much, even if we also allow the children to continue with this work at other, additional times. One really cannot afford to dabble with creative work, doing a bit here and a bit there. Creativity has to be the backbone of our work for a considerable part of the week. It is a way of school life that runs through all the activities of the children.

In most schools, however, it is necessary to timetable the use of the larger areas, such as the hall, for individual classes. This is unavoidable and as a result it becomes necessary to group the other activities round the time available for the hall so that the best use is made of the space.

Presentation

There are, of course, other points which are relevant to organization. Reference has already been made to the role of the teacher in selecting and developing the theme, and appraising the results. Throughout thematic work the teacher must try, in spite of all difficulties, to differentiate between what is honest and sincere and what is false and derivative. He is concerned with the setting of standards, above all. These standards must be high, for I think that there is a great danger that the right and proper consideration for the less gifted child may lead to an unnecessary lowering of standards generally. Teachers must not accept the shoddy, the uncared for, or anything less than the best each child can give. The answer may well be that if we get these qualities then we have failed to excite, to interest, or to create a proper ethos. This is of little comfort, of course, in a classroom situation, when confronted with a dog-eared book or tatty piece of paper. Then one is driven back to trying to lead children to care and to take a pride in their work. I suspect that the problem will always be with us, but teachers must not falter in their efforts in this direction. If we lower our standards, even in the name of an ill-conceived liberalism, we do no service to anyone. The child who is involved in thematic work should be a disciplined child, and this will reflect in all his work, be it the attempts to master a necessary skill or the expression of his thoughts and feelings.

I would hate to be doctrinaire about the form in which children present their work. In recent years there has been a remarkable growth of children making individual books, and this development, together with the folders, friezes, scattered papers on walls, and big class books, is entirely appropriate. However, we have also to be disciplined and realize that the environment with which we surround the child is probably the most vital factor in raising standards. This does not apply only to the visual environment but to the total situation. It also applies to subjects other than thematic work. For example, Vera Southgate emphasizes that the reading environment and the consequent 'reading drive in force' is the greatest factor in teaching children to read (Warbuton and V. Southgate, 1969), and Andrew Wilkinson says 'One learns language by being in a situation that calls language forth' (*Foundations of Language*). There are obviously many other examples of support for the primacy of the situation in which we put the child for his education. I firmly believe that what we put before the child must be the best available and that time and money spent on display, lettering, and so on are well spent. Presentation of work matters; care of equipment matters; handwriting, neatness, orderliness, and attention all matter, and, in fact, should be of a higher standard in a free creative atmosphere than in the drier, more formal approach. In our busy classrooms there will often be a mess, but it will be the mess of industry and not of sloth, and there is a world of difference.

Marking

Another sore question is that of marking. I think marking arises not so much
from desire to correct as from the teacher's real wish to feel that he is in
control of a situation, knows what children are doing, and is assessing progress. Teachers have to learn when to mark (and I use the word in a correc-
tive rather than a numerical sense), and when to leave alone. Some teachers
favour work done in rough, which is later copied out. In doing this we have
to be sure of what we are looking for. Spelling is not our main concern as
we assist the children to search for the right phrase, that will give an easier
flow or involve a new construction. The children will then be reconstructing
more than re-writing and the value is soon apparent. To quote Andrew
Wilkinson again, on linguistically disadvantaged children and their unaware-
ness of the possibilities of language: 'They have a jewel which is worth a
fortune, which can be worked to a rare edge of precision, which can be cut
to a many faceted beauty: and they are playing marbles with it in the backyard.' By this repolishing through knowledge of the possibilities of language
derived from talking and reading, they might at least become better marble
players.

Other teachers prepare the children for words they think will be used,
before any writing takes place, thus trying to minimize spelling errors in
advance. This practice may be restrictive, but it is an idea worth attention
from time to time. Word lists to which reference can be made, a child's own
book of special words, is a practice which helps. I myself have always found
dictionaries to be of little use as far as children's spelling in their own writing is concerned. They will simply not stop to look at them. Ideally we
should correct in the presence of the child, but this is only rarely possible,
as time is always too short.

We correct, I think, for two reasons. Firstly, to point out avoidable errors
or better constructions to the child and, secondly, to build up for ourselves
a basis of future work from what we see. In the first case I think it is vital
that children take action themselves when their work has been corrected.
They may have a special book in which to put corrected spellings, or a time
set aside to deal with them, but they must do something with the corrected
words. I have seen too much teachers' time spent on corrections that have
probably not even been noticed by the child; and who can blame him?
The younger children count their 'stars' and the older children relegate the
correction to yesterday. The second purpose has probably greater value, and
involves the teacher in keeping some kind of record which can be used to
group children having the same difficulty or to indicate the need for some
class or large group lessons. (See the books on teaching in the index.)

Even when a good situation has been set up and the children are actively engaged (perhaps all writing), many teachers are unable to resist the temptation to go round reading over shoulders, making suggestions, having children out to read—disturbing thoughts and being ever so busy when they should be sitting down minding their own business. There is a time to leave children alone and to let them get on with their work. They can sometimes manage without teachers and in the process might produce more individually honest work.

Part 2   Some themes

Children

Children enjoy exploring their own world, especially their relationships with other children and with adults. I have sub-divided this theme into three sections: *Escapades, Getting into trouble,* and *Come play with me.* These represent only part of the experience of being a child but I believe them to be a very vivid part. Teachers will wish to supplement this material by exploring other aspects of childhood experience which seem important to individuals in their classes. There must be a great deal of overlap between sections, and obviously throughout all the themes we are touching upon this experience of being a child. Because this theme so directly taps experience, the teacher should be able to learn a great deal about the children themselves as he develops the language of their situation, and helps them observe their own activities more closely. To achieve this to any satisfactory degree, the honesty of the child/teacher relationship is paramount.

I Escapades

Readings

Hiding in the Furniture Van	*On the Run* Ch.14	Nina Bawden
Laying the Charge	*Flood Warning* Ch.2	Paul Berna
The Ambush in Abbey Lane	*The Otterbury Incident* Ch.1	C. Day Lewis
The Tots in the Tower	*The Wheel on the School* Ch.4	Meindert De Jong
Searching for the Burglars	*The Children of the House* Ch.11	Brian Fairfax-Lucy and Philippa Pearce
Roland in the Ruins	*Elidor* Ch. 1	Alan Garner
The Staple Again	*The Bonnie Pit Laddie* Ch.3, 7	Frederick Grice
Through the Tunnel	*The Habit of Loving* (also in *Wordscapes*)	Doris Lessing

Robert in the Mill	*Pig in the Middle* Ch. 10	William Mayne
Pinching Staples	*There is a Happy Land* Ch.3	Keith Waterhouse
Child on Top of a Greenhouse	Theodore Roethke	*The Oxford Book of Verse for Juniors* 4; *Voices* 1; *Junior Voices* 3
Harold's Leap	Stevie Smith	*Selected Poems*
Windy Boy in a Windswept Tree	Geoffrey Summerfield	*As Large as Alone*; *Wordscapes*
The Rescue	Hal Summers	*Dawn and Dusk*; *Enjoying Poetry* 6; *Harrap's Junior Book of Modern Verse*

Movement/drama

General

1. Move as you would:
   a. Dodging from hiding-place to hiding-place in a builder's yard.
   b. Over and through various obstacles:

   a barbed wire fence (try cutting it)
   a narrow gap in a hedge
   along the top of a wall on your hands and knees; on your feet
   over a very muddy patch of ground
   along the branch of a tree
   under a fence

   c. Feeling your way with hands and feet in the dark. While you are feeling your way you hear a scurrying sound and see a rat. Show what you do.
   d. Stealing across a yard and hearing someone coming. Show what you would do. Wait until you are sure they have gone, and continue.
   e. As a watchman who thought he heard or saw someone or something, and went to investigate. Work in threes at this and develop a scene where two are children in a forbidden place and one an adult. Speak as you need to.
   f. Laying out wire for an explosive charge. Practise this as the boys did in *Flood Warning*.
2. In *On the Run* the four children work out a plan to decoy the watchman

while the others hide in the van. The same sort of thing happens in
Eric Allen's *The Latchkey Children* (Chapter 11). In groups work out
mimes for these scenes. Can you think of other scenes where a decoy
would be needed?

3. Have you ever made a dangerous leap?
    a. Leap up to catch hold of something. Catch the branch of a tree on
       which you can swing and then catch another. If you fall, try again.
       Leap down from a wall or tree. Show how you are feeling first. What
       about your landing?
    b. Creep up and leap in to surprise someone in a friendly way; in a fear-
       some way. Make suitable noises as you leap.
    c. Jump across a river using two stepping-stones and land on the bank
       on the other side.
    d. Take up a position as though you were going to jump across a ravine.
       Are you sure you can do it? Feel for your footing, work up to your
       leap, and show how you feel. Try again with different landings.
       Now you can have a run at it. Listen to the percussion roll for the
       run up and the crash for the jump. Again alter your landings.
       This time you have to land in a certain spot and keep your balance.
    e. You are in a burning room and have to leap through a window. How
       are you going to protect your body?
    f. You have to jump from a moving train; onto a moving train. Show
       how you work up to it and land each time.

Elidor

1. You are in a half-demolished building.
    a. Pick your way over rubble and through partly blocked doorways,
       across broken floors, etc.
    b. Search for a ball you have lost. You might have to lift and move things.
    c. Pick your way up a staircase. Test the steps to ensure they can take
       your weight. You may have to avoid some of them.
    d. Upstairs the floorboards have been taken up, leaving only the rafters.
       Pick your way across them.
    e. You hear a kitten in a corner upstairs. Go and resuce it and bring it
       down. How are you going to hold it? What difference will carrying
       the kitten make to your movements?
    f. Try now as though you are helping an old person up or down these
       stairs.
    g. In the building you come to an old door. Try to open it. Where does
       it lead to?

2. Work in a group of three. You go into a large, partly demolished building and become separated. Something happens to one of you. You may be injured, trapped, or make a great discovery. Talk it over and work out your group scene.

The Bonnie Pit Laddie

1. Open the door. Unscrew the hinges and lift it off. Lie on your tummy and look down the hole. In the darkness, feel your way around the hole.
2. Drop a stone down the hole to test its depth. Make sounds for when the stone lands.
3. Practise different positions for getting on to the ladder.
4. Descend into the hole on the ladder. Start from where you get on it. Remember it is dark, the ladder is old, and you are frightened.
5. Come back up again and dust off your clothes. Try to show how you are feeling.
6. Go down the ladder as though you were leading someone, directing their feet, and encouraging them.
7. Try coming up as if you were carrying something.
8. Go down again as Dick did, hampered by his lamp.
9. Work with a partner. One go down first while the other watches, then the first one shine his light to help the other.
10. You are going down the ladder when it breaks or comes away from the wall. Show what happens as you fall, lose consciousness, and come again. Are you injured at all?
11. Be the old miner at work in his cavil. The space is cramped and you have to pick, lever, and load your coal. Try working in different positions on a narrow face.
12. Work with a partner and develop the scene where Dick and Kit go through the workings, which get narrower, more obstructed, and more difficult until you see the old miner at work. Get in position to watch him.
13. Work in threes, one to be the miner and the others Dick and Kit. Talk it over first to decide your paths, using as much space as you can. Action is going on all the time. Start from where Dick falls and the boys set off, and include the part where the miner comes back to find his pick gone while the boys make their escape.

(*The extracts mentioned from* On the Run, There is a Happy Land, The Wheel on the School, *and* Otterbury Incident *can all be developed along similar lines.*)

Written work

1. Write the story of 'The Rescue' as if you were the boy, the father, or the mother.
2. Have you ever rescued something? Tell about it.
3. Have you ever taken a great risk to do something, or finally done something of which you were very afraid? Write about it.
4. Write about any time you have been dared to do something.
5. Write a description of a demolition site.
6. You were Dick. What was it like going down the staple?
7. Tell about any time you were scared and had to hold on to something tightly. What was it like when it was all over?
8. Can you remember any time when you went into a forbidden place? What did it feel like?
9. Have you ever followed your brother or sister anywhere? Did they mind you coming? Tell the story.
10. Outline the story of your decoy plan for **General**, 2.
11. In *Elidor*, 1.g you came to an old door and tried to open it. Describe how you come upon it and what you find.
12. Have you ever been high up anywhere? Tell what it was like.
13. Describe any escapade you and your pals have been involved in.
14. Can you write an imaginary story about a gang meeting where an escapade is planned? (Read 'Operation Glazier', *Otterbury Incident*, Chapter 4, and *The Adventures of Huckleberry Finn,* Chapter 2.)

II Getting into trouble

Readings

Broken Window	*The Otterbury Incident* End Ch. 1, Ch. 2	C. Day Lewis
The Scorpions in the Matchbox	*My Family and Other Animals* Ch. 9	Gerald Durrell
Events in Garnet's Life	*Thimble Summer* Ch. 7	Elizabeth Enright
The Job that Went Wrong	*The Family from One End Street* Ch. 2	Eve Garnett
Dick and Kit before the Headmaster	*The Bonnie Pit Laddie* Ch. 1, 8	Frederick Grice
Losing Things	*Emil and the Detectives* Ch. 5	Erich Kastner
Helping Father Pack	*The Wind on the Moon* Ch. 1	Eric Linklater

Tommy Loses his Half-Sovereign	*Circus Boy* Ch. 5	Ruth Manning-Sanders
Trouble with the Codfish	*Sand* Ch. 5	William Mayne
David	Eleanor Farjeon	*The Children's Bells*
A Song About Myself	John Keats	*The Faber Book of Children's Verse; Poetry Panorama* 3; *Birthright Poetry* 1; *The Oxford Book of Verse for Juniors* 1; *The Merry-Go-Round; All Day Long*
Noise	J. Pope	*Blackwell's Junior Poetry Book* 3

Movement/drama

1. Move as you would:
    a. When a window is broken and you don't want to know anything about it. You are all innocence.
    b. Trying to sneak in when you are late home.
    c. Trying to repair the damage after dirtying your best clothes.
    d. When owning up to something you have done.
    e. When you have been sent for and know it means trouble.
    f. Finding yourself shut in a forbidden place.
    g. Listening to something that means trouble for you.
    h. Throwing stones at a target, when one goes off course and ... crash!
    i. Doing a job that goes wrong—soot falling down the chimney, burning the baking, flooding the kitchen, etc.
2. Do you get into trouble for making too much noise? Be an adult listening to a din for as long as you can before quietening it.
    Go through some of the ways you try to talk in class without being seen.
3. Be Emil asleep in the carriage. Wake up and find your money gone.
4. Act through the scene where Tommy finds his money has gone. You are going to produce it proudly at first (it might be in another pocket or have dropped on the floor). Turn out your things to look for it and go back up the road searching for it. Work with a partner and add the innkeeper. Make up a dialogue to go with this scene.
5. Can you think of a situation where you break something of value to someone else? Do it accidentally; on purpose. In both cases, realize it means trouble and show what you will do.

6. *Events in Garnet's life.* Make a list of all the ways Mr. Freebody had helped Garnet. Be Mr. Freebody:

   a. Getting the safety pin out of her mouth.

   Imagine you see a child sucking something and get suspicious. How will you get her to open her mouth without swallowing? Be very gentle when you discover what it is.

   Work with a partner who will be the child. Speak with her and go through the scene.

   b. Hauling her out of the creek. Try this in different ways:

   from the bank, a ridge, a boat

   using a pole or a rope

   holding onto a branch

   jumping in and wading out.

   When you have rescued the child, show what you are going to do next.

   c. Getting her down from a tree.

   d. Rescuing her from the bull. See the bull before the child does and show how you will act if the bull is

   taking no notice

   looking round suspiciously

   getting ready to charge

   charging

   e. Picking her up after being tossed by the heifer. Make sure no bones are broken before you move her. Try different ways of lifting her and carrying her home.

You can now put these together into an episodic class drama. Split up into groups and decide which events you will show.

How are the episodes to be linked together? You might need a commentator, or perhaps it could be done as an interviewer with Garnet who recalls the events of her earlier life in a television programme. Work out a script for this interview.

Written work

1. Write a story about the day everything went wrong.
2. Have you ever been blamed for something which you thought would be a good turn? Tell about it.
3. David in Eleanor Farjeon's poem gets into trouble for throwing stones. What do you get into trouble for most? Make a list of some of your good and bad points.

4. What things have happened in your life like Garnet's? Write about them.
5. Tell the story of the time you broke something.
6. Is there any difference between getting into trouble at home and getting into trouble at school? Explain the difference.
7. Mr. Freebody said all children get into mischief. Do all adults feel like this? Write about adults and children in trouble.
8. What does your mother get most cross with you about?
9. Write about one of the events in Garnet's life as if you were Mr Freebody.
10. Can you think what it feels like when you get into trouble? Is it always the same feeling? Do you resolve to do better, then ... ?
11. Describe the time when you were in most trouble.
12. Do you know you are in trouble from the way someone calls to you or looks at you? What goes through your mind then?

III Come play with me (in the street)

Readings

Counting Strides	*The Latchkey Children* Ch. 1	Eric Allen
First Riding a Bicycle	*The Four Storey Mistake* Ch. 4	Elizabeth Enright
Spit Nolan	*The Goalkeeper's Revenge and other stories*	Bill Naughton
Hiddy Games	*There is a Happy Land* Ch. 6	Keith Waterhouse
Street Games (Ted and Me)	*There is a Happy Land* Ch. 1	Keith Waterhouse
Going Downhill on a Bicycle: A Boy's Song	Henry Charles Beeching	*Enjoying Poetry* 4
Child's Bouncing Song	Tony Connor	*Voices* 1
You can't catch me	Eleanor Farjeon	*Round the Day*
Urchin	Christopher Hassall	*Round the Day*
The Birthright	E. Lewis	*All Day Long*; *Exploring Poetry* 4
Tom Tom	Phyllis McGinley	*Round the Day*
Mulga Bill's Bicycle	A. B. Paterson	*Mood and Rhythm* 2
Hard Cheese	Justin St John	*Junior Voices* 3
Hide and Seek	Vernon Scannell	*Junior Voices* 4; *Happenings* 1; *Wordscapes*; *Enjoying Poetry* 2

From 'Paper Boats'	Rabindranath Tagore	*All Day Long*; *A Flock of Words*
Song for a Ball Game	Wilfrid Thorley	*Rhyme and Rhythm* (blue); *Exploring Poetry* 1; *Poetry Panorama* 2

Movement/drama

1. Play an imaginary game of 'pig in the middle' where two of you keep the ball from the third player.
2. Play 'tig' or 'catch' with an imaginary companion.
3. Move as you would going along a street avoiding the cracks on the pavement. 'If you tread on a nick ...'
4. Bounce an imaginary ball to any rhyme you know. Try to make a pattern on the floor with your bouncing.

   Now do something else with some part of your body as you bounce and include this in your floor pattern.

   Learn part of one of the bouncing songs you have heard and move to that. Make up one of your own. Start with a simple phrase—'my mother said ...' Say it to yourself in as many ways as you can, then do the bouncing to it, and see if you can carry it further.

   If not, carry on bouncing to that phrase said differently, with different emphasis, speed, and so on, and other words will come. Try again beginning with people's names, jobs, foods, or any other phrase you can think of.
5. Work with a partner and do the sort of things that the two boys did in *There is a Happy Land*, changing games as you go along. You can keep to their games if you like or work out a sequence of your own. Notice how easily they moved from one to the other. Take it in turns to be the leader and speak as you need to.

Written work

1. Read 'The Birthright' by E. Lewis. What advantage do town children have over country children?
2. If you moved either to or from the town, what part of your play would you miss most?
3. Write out a collection of bouncing or skipping rhymes.
4. How do children's games alter from time to time during the year? Write a calendar of your games.

5. What games do you play alone when going along the street?
6. Make a poem about 'Marbles' or 'Conkers'.
7. Do you play 'knock and run'? Write about this game as if you were a person inside the house.
8. What other games do you play which annoy people?
9. Is there any particular street or area in which you play often? What is special about this place?
10. Describe some of the games your parents have told you they played as children.
11. Do your games sometimes end badly? Tell about games you have started but that have just died out.
12. Write about your favourite game.
13. Do you play out at night? What do you play when the street lights are lit? Is it different to playing in daylight?
14. Could you invent an 'argy bargy' language of your own? Write out a simple passage using your language. Try to say it and apply it to other sentences.
15. Have you ever made a 'bogey' or used pram wheels for games in the street? Explain what you made. Draw sketches to make the description clearer.
16. What do you do to entertain a young child whom you have to take out or care for?

III Come play with me (in the park)

Readings

	The Latchkey Children	Eric Allen
Reminiscences of Childhood	*Quite Early One Morning*	Dylan Thomas
Birches	Robert Frost	*Happenings* 1; *Selected Poems*
The Swing	Mary I. Osborn	*Enjoying Poetry* 5; *The Book of a Thousand Poems*
The Swing	R.L. Stevenson	*Enjoying Poetry* 5
Evening in the Park	John Walsh	*The Roundabout by the Sea*
Races	Humbert Wolfe	*The Oxford Book of Verse for Juniors* 1.

Movement/drama

1. Be an adult in a park:
   >watching boys playing football
   >pushing a swing
   >trying to stop a roundabout
   >encouraging a child to come down a slide
   >walking round a playground, watching what is going on and
   >doing different things.
2. Practise getting a swing up as high as you can. Make the sounds to go
   with it. Work as a group of children on a line of swings.
3. Work with a partner on an imaginary see-saw. Add a third person
   standing in the middle and weighting the see-saw.
4. Work in a group.
   a. You are a rocking boat. Make your boat and rock it. Talk it over first
   to decide how each person is going to move to show a different part
   of the boat's movement.
   b. Make a roundabout shape and move as one body. Let other children
   come, get off and on your roundabout, and help it to go faster.
   c. Make a 'jungle jim' using your arms, legs, and bodies, to make spaces
   for other children to use.
5. Let's act a playground scene. Talk it over first to decide what equipment
   there is going to be and where it is to be positioned. Let some be equipment and others children playing on or with it.

Written work

1. Describe any person you see regularly in your park.
2. How do you judge a tree? Try to describe the best tree you have ever
   seen or played in. Would you like to make a tree house?
3. Which thing do you go for first in the playground? Make up a poem
   about this, telling which thing always attracts you.
4. Corporations are always proud of their parks. Are you? What would you
   put in a park or playground if you had the chance to design one?
5. Make up a poem of your own about swings, see-saws, or slides. Try to
   get the pattern of the poem to match the feeling they give you.
6. Tell which part of your park, other than the playground, excited you
   most.
7. Which is the best park you have ever been in?
8. What does it feel like to run in a race? Think of the start, running, and
   the ending. You might not win but ... Write a poem telling about yourself in a race.

9. Write a poem called 'Playgrounds'. What would you hear and see there?

III Come play with me (on the beach)

Readings

East Anglian Bathe	John Betjeman	*The Albemarle Book of Modern Verse* 1; *All Day Long*
maggie and milly and molly and may	e. e. cummings	*Happenings* 1
The Pool in the Rock	Walter de la Mare	*Poetry and Life* 3
The Sea-shell	Amy Lowell	*Poetry and Life* 3; *Mood and Rhythm* 1; *All Day Long*
Beech Leaves	James Reeves	*All Day Long; Wordscapes; Poetry Panorama* 3
The Shell	James Stephens	*Enjoying Poetry* 5; *Rhyme and Rhythm* (yellow); *All Day Long; The Book of a Thousand Poems; A Flock of Words*
Shrimping	Ian Serraillier	*Happily Ever After*
Beach Burial	John Walsh	*The Roundabout by the Sea; Wordscapes*
Down to the Sea	John Walsh	*The Truants*
First Dip	John Walsh	*The Roundabout by the Sea*
The Sand Castle	John Walsh	*The Truants*
The Shell	Mary Webb	*All Day Long*

Movement/drama

1. Get into a position to watch a rock pool. See all the life inside it. Put your hand in gently to remove a stone. Does anything happen? Watch any one creature as it moves in the pool. If it disappears, wait until it is there again or you see something else. Move about the pool as you need to, taking up fresh watching positions. Try to catch something with your hand. Try with a net.
2. Shut your eyes. Listen to all the sounds you can hear in the room. Try to pick them out and identify them. Pick out one sound. Listen to that.

Can you hear yourself breathing?

Listen to the silence. Shut out all other sounds.

Put an imaginary shell to your ear—can you hear the sound?

3. Move as you would on the beach looking for shells, stones, weed, and fish. Pick up the things, using different movements and speeds. Feel them and look at them. Keep some if you wish.

4. Take a shower. Show when the water is hot or cold and when it changes. Make it cold. How do you feel when you come out?

Move now the way you would in sea water. Feel it as it goes over your toes, up to your tummy, as a wave comes and splashes over you. Immerse yourself in the water and splash it all over yourself.

Play a game in the water with a partner.

Come out as you would to dry yourself.

Go into the sea again:

    scrambling over the rocks

    going over a shingly beach

    crossing a patch where there are many jellyfish before you reach the sea.

5. Work out mimes of these people on a beach.

    a. A parent with a baby in a push-chair and lots of other gear to carry.

    b. Opening a deck-chair. Make a comic mime of this.

    c. Donkey men.

    d. An adult trying to sun-bathe and being annoyed by a dog.

    e. Adults on a rather cool beach.

    f. A very busy ice-cream man.

    g. A fisherman.

6. Let me see you working on the beach:

    levelling off a spot to sit on

    damming up a stream

    digging a channel

    making a sand castle

    covering someone with sand or stones

7. Body shapes.

    a. Rocks. Think carefully of the shape of rocks and put your body into a rock shape. Make it smooth. Make it rough and jagged. Make some parts smooth and others jagged. Practise a pattern of moving from one rock shape to another.

    Work in a group and make a rock scene with your bodies. Try to have some different shapes and heights moulded together. Can you get the idea of a pool in your rocks?

b. Sea creatures. Practise these body shapes in as many ways as you can:

a limpet ⎱
a barnacle ⎰ gripping with different parts of your body
a crab
a jellyfish
a starfish

Set up a large rock scene as you did before. This time some children are going to be sea creatures and cling to the rocks like limpets and barnacles. It may help if you practise clinging to another child's rock shape before you go into a group.

Written work

1. Write a poem about going into the sea to bathe.
2. You are on a crowded beach and it starts to rain. What happens? How does it all look after a few minutes?
3. Write about the beach as it appears to you early in the morning or in the evening.
4. What is the worst part of being on a beach?
5. Write a poem on 'Sand Castles', perhaps ending with the tide coming in and sucking the castle away.
6. In his poem 'Beech Leaves' James Reeves tells of a boy kicking and striding in the leaves. How do you feel as you kick and stride in the sea?
7. Tell of anything that has ever happened to you on a beach.
8. Where do you like to play on the beach you go to most often? Are you always allowed to go there?
9. Describe how one of these things—noise, smells, colour, litter—is special on beaches.

III Come play with me (with the gang)

Readings

Clio and the Committee	*A Handful of Thieves* Ch. 2	Nina Bawden
The Battle	*Knights of the Cardboard Castle* Ch. 10	Elizabeth Beresford
The Peace of Otterbury	*The Otterbury Incident* Ch. 3	C. Day Lewis

Michael Gets Sworn In	*Pig in the Middle* Ch.2	William Mayne
'L' for Leader	*Plot Night* Ch. 4, 5	William Mayne
Tom Sawyer's Gang	*The Adventures of Huckleberry Finn* Ch.2	Mark Twain

Written work

1. Have you ever been in a gang? Tell about it—where you met and what you did.
2. Describe what you think would be the perfect gang meeting-place.
3. Make up an oath which every member of your gang would have to swear to.
4. Write an imaginary account of the children in a rival gang.
5. Is there a real rival gang to yours? Write about it.

Parents, Home and Family

The approach to this theme will vary according to the age of the classes involved. Older children, in particular, are helped by the awareness that ambivalent feelings to home and family life, feelings of love and frustration, security and tension, joy and sadness, are not just experienced by them alone, but are common to all of us. As they search for ways of understanding their experience, any work which helps to make this more intelligible, and perhaps more bearable, is of value. The passages of literature are chosen with the hope of deepening their insight into the complex relationship of family life. Discussion is vital if any depth is to be achieved. This should range widely over the common ground of family relationships: the attitudes of parents and children to each other; other members' needs and aims; freedoms and restrictions; privacy; praise and blame; private and shared property and interests. Some of these discussions will arise out of drama practices, some from the readings, and some will develop out of other discussions. All such talk needs to be very carefully handled by the teacher. Nothing can be forced, and all observations are valid.

Readings

My Family	*Over the Bridge* Ch.1	Richard Church
Tio Pao Finds his Parents	*The House of Sixty Fathers* Ch.9	Meindert De Jong
Mother	*Cider with Rosie* Ch.7	Laurie Lee
Father and Son	*Avalanche!* end of Ch.4	A. Rutgers van der Loeff
My Aunt and Uncle	*Kipps* Ch. 1	H. G. Wells
The Parable of the Prodigal Son	*The Holy Bible* Luke 15; 11−32	
Jesus Lost in the Temple	*The Holy Bible* Luke 2; 42−50	

The Mother's Song	Anon.	*Voices* 3
The Father's Song	Anon.	*Voices* 1
Our Mother	Anon.	*The Book of a Thousand Poems*
'My mother said, I never should ...'	Anon.	*Poetry and Life* 2; *Exploring Poetry* 2; *The Oxford Book of Poetry for Children*
To My Mother	George Barker	*A Flock of Words*
Blaming Sons	T'ao Ch'ien	*Voices* 2
Brother	Robert Graves	*Voices* 2
Jesus and his Mother	Thom Gunn	*Penguin New Poetry*
A Helping Hand	Miroslav Holub	*Selected Poems*
My Brother Bert	Ted Hughes	*Meet My Folks!; Rhyme and Rhythm* (green)
My Sister Jane	Ted Hughes	*Meet My Folks!; Rhyme and Rhythm* (yellow); *A Flock of Words*
My Father	Ted Hughes	*Voices* 1
My Grandpa	Ted Hughes	*Meet My Folks!*
Ask Daddy, He Won't Know	Ogden Nash	*The Albemarle Book of Modern Verse* 1
Social Studies	M. Neville	*Junior Voices* 2
Morning Glory	Michell Raper	*Wordscapes*
What's the matter up here? ...	C. Sandburg	*Junior Voices* 2
A Father's Advice to His Son	William Shakespeare	*Hamlet*, Act I, Sc.3; *Enjoying Poetry* 3
Guilty Conscience	Rodney Sivyour	*Thoughtshapes*
If I Should Ever By Chance	Edward Thomas	*The Pattern of Poetry; The Faber Book of Children's Verse; The Oxford Book of Poetry for Children*
The One Furrow	R.S. Thomas	*Song at The Year's Turning*
Taking Out Jim	John Walsh	*The Roundabout by the Sea*

Movement/drama

General

1. Move as you would:
    as a child being sent to bed early
    scolding your child
    being told off by your parents
    clearing up your room
    looking for something you have lost
    trying to get your children in from play
    nursing, feeding, playing with the baby
    trying to teach the baby to walk, speak, tie a bow
    helping your father clean the car, work in the garden, do any job
    showing your child how to sew, play any game, use a knife and
    fork, or something you can remember being shown yourself.

2. Be your mother or father at home doing something. Show clearly what
   you are doing.
   Something happens:
    someone comes to the door to sell something
    a welcome visitor, whom you have not seen for a long time,
    arrives unexpectedly
    someone neither of you wants to see arrives
    one of you breaks something, or something in the house goes
    wrong.

   Decide what it is going to be, then act out the event, perhaps taking up
   what you were doing afterwards. How did you feel about the interrup-
   tion?
   Do the scene again, showing a different response to the disturbance.

3. Work in pairs as sisters, brothers, or brother and sister. Play a game
   together. Let something happen during the game:
    you fall and break an arm, or cut yourself badly
    your partner throws a ball that breaks a window
    you are interrupted by some children you don't like

you disagree about what you are playing, or how to play it

your parents interrupt to ask you to do something unpleasant.

Talk it over until you are sure what is going to happen, think how you
will feel about it, and act it through.

Add a parent to the scene. What is going to happen now? Try the scene
as many ways as possible, taking different parts.

The prodigal son

I aim here to produce a class or large group drama on this story. It is a
great parable, showing many sides of human nature, all of which can provide a stimulus for individual work, and later for group work, when the
story is woven into a coherent whole. The teacher must try to give all the
children as wide as possible a range of experience in acting out the different
emotions, ideas, and relationships in the story, before embarking on any
attempt to produce a finished 'play'. The child's early individual practices
are largely subjective—he is exploring the ideas of the subject for himself
and with himself. Later he can transfer these findings to the more objective
field of working with others, responding to their ideas and gaining much
from the discipline that structured group work demands. In many ways
what I suggest is a 'theatre workshop' approach, and as such the flow of
ideas and the direction the work takes must come from the participants,
although the function of the teacher is still to stimulate and to suggest
fresh approaches.

Unfortunately, the parts which are easiest in the dramatic sense are not
those which, I think, mean most to the story. Special attempts should be
made, and situations may have to be devised, to help the children understand
the elder brother's part and the dominant theme of the father's love for
both his children, which is expressed so differently for each child. I hope
that the teacher will select from the suggestions below on the basis of his
own feelings and the needs of his own class. The parable is particularly
suitable for work with 9 to 13 year olds, and can also be placed in a
modern context.

Leaving

1. How do you think the younger son went to ask his father for his share
   of the property? Practise waiting outside a room, and entering to make
   your request, in as many different ways as you can. Persuasion, anger,
   fear, timidity, nervousness, and greed all come into it.
   Come out:
   a. As though you have been unsuccessful.
   b. As though you have been successful. Start to prepare for your journey
      to the city. Put the words in, perhaps gradually as you act it through.
      Try to make sure your words and movements fit together.
2. Be the younger son working on the farm or in the fields. How do you
   think he was feeling? Do you think it was easy for him to decide to ask

his father for his share? Decide what jobs you are doing and show by
the way you are working what you think about it all. Determine to go
and see your father and try the scene you have previously practised in 1.
Do it differently until you have got the best approach. Watch each other
and see if you can tell how the other person is feeling.

3. Say this phrase 'I'm getting out of here' as many ways as you can. Practise another phrase for the younger son. Now try with a reply: 'Yes, I
   would if I were you'.
   Put these phrases together yourself. Work with a partner with these
   phrases or others you can think of, exploring all the ways of saying them.

4. Do you think the elder brother worked differently from the younger
   brother? Be the elder brother at his work. How do you think they got
   on together while they were working? Work with a partner and try to
   develop a scene which leads to the younger brother going off to see his
   father. Add this to the scene you have already done in 1.

5. Be the elder brother as a rather sly character encouraging his brother to
   go, listening to what happens with the father, and watching him leave
   the farm, which he now thinks will all be his.

6. All be the father. What might he think when his son comes in. Walk
   about as the father would, stop, and turn when you hear someone come
   in. Speak and show what you are like. Try it several times in different
   ways.

7. Put these scenes together now in groups. One be the father, two be the
   brothers, and the others be farm workers seeing and hearing what goes
   on. Is there room for a mother?

In the city

Work out short mimes for these:

1. You are the younger brother arriving in the big city and seeing all the
   unaccustomed sights.
   Now be a person who sees him arriving and plots to get some of his
   money, not by force but by trickery (read Alan Paton's *Cry the Beloved
   Country*, Chapter 4, for an example of this situation).

2. Be the younger brother:
   a. Fitting himself out with spanking new clothes.
   b. Furnishing his rooms. See the room and tell a partner what you are
      going to get.
   c. Gambling. Play all sorts of games. You win and lose.
   d. Wining, dining, and having a gay old time.
   e. Meeting a crowd of new 'friends' and treating them all. Work as a

group with one as the son and the others as 'friends'. How do you
think they regard him?

   f. Waking up one morning and searching for his money. There is:
      plenty left yet
      not much, but it doesn't matter
      nothing left at all.

3. *a.* As the younger brother, you wake up one morning, hear a knock at
the door, and realize it is someone to whom you owe money or someone who is going to throw you out. How are you going to act? Talk
over what you might do and try as many ways as you can.

   b. Be in a group of three who have gone to collect the debt or evict the
son. Talk it over and work out the scene and what you are going to
say and do.

   c. Put *a.* and *b.* together.

4. Be the son again:

   a. Trying to raise money, selling some of your goods for the best price
you can, borrowing from a past friend, begging in the street or a public
place, doing any menial job. If it were the present day, what sort of
job might this be?

   b. Finally deciding to go home. Work up to this in the scene where you
mind the pigs.

Returning

Put together some of the work you have done so far. Mark out different
parts of the floor as 'city' and 'farm'. There may be several of each to
accommodate all the action. The 'city' will have the people doing some of
the things you have practised in the last section, and the farm will have the
father, older son, and some workers. Take no notice of the other group but
try to realize that they are there.

Do you think the younger son ever thought of home while he was away
or the family ever wondered about him? Show this in your movement.
Remember that the time spent must have been quite long and we should
get some contrast between life in the city and on the farm. Signals for
dawn and sunset may help to give a sense of time passing.

Work in groups with everyone involved in some way. Keep action of
some sort going, but if you finish, just sit and watch; you may be able to
join in again.

1. *a.* Be a worker on the farm. See the younger son approach, and rush off
to tell the father. Work with a partner, one to be the worker, and one
to be the father, who will get the message, see his son, give out his

orders, and go to meet him. How are you, as the father, going to
watch him approach, and greet him?

    b. Work in threes, one to be the son approaching, one the father, and
one a servant. Work through this scene.

2. All be servants preparing for the party. There will be plenty to do.
All do something, and then something different.

3. Work with a partner, one to be the servant preparing for the party and
one to be the older son returning tired from the field. Practise each part
and work out your dialogue.

4. In pairs now practise the last scene between the father and the older son.
This might be difficult and there are many ways to approach it. First
examine these approaches, and watch each other, before you begin
yourself.

5. Now have the party. You can be whoever you like. There will be
musicians playing, people singing, dancing, eating, drinking. You might
prefer to be one of the family. What do you think their attitude would be?

(*From this first attempt it will be possible to separate the various groups in
order to organize them all as a class in a final party scene. There should not
be too much roistering if the feeling is to be kept.*)

Written work

1. Ted Hughes makes up some fine nonsense poems about his family.
See if you can do the same. What sort of unlikely job can you think of
for your father, brother, sister, or mother?

2. In 'The Father's Song' an Eskimo father prays for his family. What do you
think your father hopes and prays for you?

3. Read 'The One Furrow' by R. S. Thomas. Is this at all similar to the
parable of the prodigal son? How do you think you will look back on
your early life?

4. Put yourself in the position of your parents on special occasions
(e.g. Christmas Eve, Bonfire Night, Open Day at school). Do they enjoy
it? Do they seem different then? Are there other times when your parents have seemed different? Tell about it.

5. Edward Thomas tells what he would do if he should ever by chance
grow rich. Say in verse or prose what you would really like to do if you
were rich.

6. Listen to the tales your mother or father tells you about their youth and
write a portrait of one of them as they were then. A photograph will
help.

7. How often do they say 'When I was your age ...'? Write a piece with that as a title.
8. Have you ever felt particularly close to your parents, as Tio Pao or Richard Church did?
9. Families are crowded places. D.H. Lawrence said that he liked people quite well

> If they will only leave me alone
> I can still have the illusion that there is room
> enough in the world.
>
> ('People', *Every Man Will Shout*)

What things do you like sharing with your family, and what do you like keeping to yourself? How do you get to be alone in your family?
10. How do you think the two brothers in the story of the prodigal son felt about each other? Is this usual for brothers? I suppose it is alright for you to quarrel with your brother, but what if anyone else does?
11. Do you think the father was right to give the son his share? Tell the story from the father's point of view.
12. What about the elder brother? How does he appeal to you, have you any sympathy for him, or is he too much of a 'goody-goody'? Do you like him? Write a portrait of him.
13. Write as though you were the younger son arriving in the big city from your quiet place in the country. Think of the excitement you felt and tell the story of your arrival. (Read Alan Paton's *Cry the Beloved Country*, Chapter 4).
14. Have you ever had to own up to yourself for making a great mistake? Think of something you have done about which you felt terrible, although perhaps no one else knew. Write an honest account of it now.
15. Describe your own home, not what it looks like, but what it means to you. Robert Frost says

> Home is the place where, when you have to go there,
> They have to take you in.
>   I should have called it
> Something you somehow haven't to deserve.
>
> ('The Death of the Hired Man', *Selected Poems*)

What makes home important to you? Later in life you might leave it— what will you remember most, do you think?
16. W.B. Yeats wrote a prayer for his daughter. If you had a son or daughter what would you wish for them?

17. Children often say 'It isn't fair ...' Just *what* isn't fair in your family?
18. Does your father understand what you are doing at school? Do you ask Daddy and find he doesn't know? How does he behave then? Why?
19. Put yourself in your mother's position. Of all the things you have ever done, what do you think she will remember?
20. Write a poem 'I mustn't ...'
21. Which are the best or worst sorts of evenings spent at home? Write an account of the evening when everything went right or everything went wrong.
22. Which things in your home, or the people who live in it, make you angry? Some of them you will not be able to change and have to learn to live with, but some you may be able to change. Which are they?
23. Are there any special things about your family—sounds, sights, smells—that make it different from other families?

People

The world of literature, both children's and adult's, is a world of people. Children's play shows how they identify with the characters they have met through books and other media. On these grounds, **People** would seem to be a fruitful topic even for quite young children. The readings are drawn from both fantasy and reality, and the children will also base their writing on their own imaginings as well as their actual experience. The children must be personally involved in their writing for it to have any meaning, and to achieve this the teacher must introduce fresh aspects of the material for the children to respond to. They may then begin to understand and fully appreciate the subject. Anything else leads to the sort of triviality which arises from the 'Describe a tramp' exercises so abundant in textbooks. The paragraphs on 'overacting' in Part I (p.24) are relevant here.

Readings

Dodder	*The Little Grey Men* Ch. 1	'B.B.'
Cocky Wainwright	*Sammy Going South* Ch. 18	W. H. Canaway
Miss Haversham	*Great Expectations* Ch. 7	Charles Dickens
The Strange Boy	*The Summer Birds* Ch. 1	Penelope Farmer
Colonel Plugg	*Chancy and the Grand Rascal* Ch. 2	Sid Fleischman
Captain Scratch	*The Ghost in the Noonday Sun* Ch. 1	Sid Fleischman
Black Jack and Mrs. Gorgandy	*Black Jack* Ch. 1	Leon Garfield
A Shepherd of the Downs	*A Shepherd's Life* Ch. 4	W. H. Hudson
Granny Billings	*The Hungry Cloud* Ch. 12	Tom Ingram

The Robber Man	*Emil and the Detectives* Ch. 3	Erich Kästner
Crabby	*Cider with Rosie* Ch. 13	Laurie Lee
Ranofer Follows Gebu	*The Golden Goblet* Ch. 10	E. J. McGraw
	Man of Everest	Tenzing Norgay
The Sevillano	*The Black Pearl* Ch. 3	Scott O'Dell
Dad	*Finn's Folly* Ch. 1	Ivan Southall
Pansy and the Herbalist	*The Workhouse Child* Ch. 8	Geraldine Symons
Bilbo Baggins	*The Hobbit*	J.R.R. Tolkien
The Stranger	*The Intruder* Ch. 2	J.R. Townsend
Huckleberry Finn	*The Adventures of Tom Sawyer* Ch.6	Mark Twain

The Prologue from 'The Canterbury Tales'	Geoffrey Chaucer	*A Flock of Words*
Tell me not here	A.E. Housman	*Collected Poems*
Japanese Children	J. Kirkup	*A Flock of Words*
Mr. Bleaney	Philip Larkin	*Penguin New Poetry*
The Sphere of Glass	John Lehmann	*The Penguin Book of Contemporary Verse; The Sphere of Glass*
The Street Musician	James Reeves	*Poetry Panorama* 2; *Mood and Rhythm* 4
The Cries of Evening	Stephen Spender	*Collected Poems*
Danny Murphy	James Stephens	*The Oxford Book of Verse for Juniors* 3; *The Book of a Thousand Poems; Blackwell's Junior Poetry Book* 3
An Old Man	R.S. Thomas	*The Pattern of Poetry*
Farm Child	R.S. Thomas	*A Flock of Words; Dawn and Dusk*

Movement/drama

General situations

a. You are hurrying up a busy street. Avoid obstacles and other people as you move. What happens when you want to pass someone and can't, or when you bump into them? Think up a situation where you

are trying to get through a door when someone else is coming the
other way loaded with luggage?
b. Take a stroll on a nice evening. Stop and look.
c. Wait for someone. Try to show how you are feeling at having to wait.
d. Go up a muddy lane.
e. Go up a shopping street. Look in the shop windows as you pass. You
come to a window round which a crowd has gathered. Try to get
into a position to see what is going on.
f. You are in a busy place and think you recognize someone in front of
you. You want to meet him. Show what you do.
Suppose it was not the person you thought it was. What happens
then?
Suppose it was someone you want to avoid. What would you do?

Particular situations
1. Be a private detective following a suspect. How are you going to move?
A tap on the cymbal means he has stopped or turned round. What are
you going to do? (Read *The Golden Goblet*, Chapter 10.)
2. Be the person who is being followed. Your suspicions grow; what do
you do?
3 Work in pairs on 1. and 2. Try to make your movements and actions fit
in with the other person's. Move about the whole hall.
4. Be a soldier moving over a minefield. Test the ground carefully before
you step about. Use a mine detector to 'sweep' the ground. What happens
if you find a mine? Work very carefully to uncover it. You now have to
make it safe. Look at it carefully and get into a good position to do
your job. Use only your fingers to start with and feel all over it. You
come to a small screw which needs loosening. Make sure your screw-
driver goes exactly where you want it to and does not slip. Does the
screw move easily? You will have to use other tools such as drills, cutters,
pliers. When you do, be certain to be in perfect control of them.
5. Be a policeman:
   walking his beat at night—testing doors, using his torch, and so on
   controlling a crowd
   directing traffic—come to a traffic jam and sort it out.
6. Move like an old person.
Let's think about different parts of an old person's body:
a. Look at your hand. Let it slowly change into an old person's hand.
Try to fasten a button with your old hand. Try other fine jobs.
b. Your eyes are going to change into an old person's eyes. Let them

change slowly. Blink them. Try to see something in the distance; read something close at hand.

   c. Shake your back. Make it move loosely in as many ways as you can. Now move your back as an older person would. Try bending down for something; wriggling through a narrow space; reaching up to lift something down.

   d. As the cymbal rolls, old age is going to spread through your body from the top of your head to the tip of your toes. Feel it come slowly to all parts of your body, and then move as an old person again.

   Use some of the situations in **General Situations** as an old person.

7. Work in pairs helping an older person to do something. Talk it over first to decide what you are going to do, then act it through.

Imaginary situations

1. Some part of your body is injured. Walk or move to show clearly which part is affected. Change the injury and walk or move again. Try to devise a situation where you would get this injury (falling, being trapped, being caught in an avalanche, hurt in an accident) and act it out. Keep the situation as simple as possible to begin with, in order to highlight the injury and the problem of moving with it.

2. Move as you would when helping someone who is injured. Show by your movement which part of his body is hurt. Try with different parts. Work with a partner, one to be injured, the other to help him.
(Only when children have had considerable experience in these practices should we move on to the next section.)

3. Pick out one of the characters you have heard or read about, and move as you think he would, doing the things he would be doing. Through discussion, try to change the character's situation, and try moving again.

Written work

1. At its earliest level this could begin with descriptions of 'a person I know'. If worthwhile results are to be obtained from this type of writing, then a chance to highlight the features that are to be written about must be given in movement/drama or craft activities. I do not think we want a general portrait, rather we want the child to recognize his awareness of some special feature which distinguishes the person from others, and to communicate this feeling. The examples from 'Canterbury Tales' in *A Flock of Words* can be very rewarding.

2. Possibly in dealing with this topic, with older children particularly, the greatest need of the child is to recognize himself. They are not too young to feel the realization of dreams, or the failure to realize them. Philip Larkin's 'Mr. Bleaney' might well highlight this.

Read:

> Stephen Spender's 'The Cries of Evening'
> A. E. Housman's 'Tell me not here'
> John Lehmann's 'The Sphere of Glass'
> R. S. Thomas' 'Farm Child'
> Tensing Norgay's *Man of Everest*

These show how adults feel about themselves and others.
How do you feel about yourself? What have you failed or succeeded in?
Tell about it.

3. You are one of the characters you have heard about. Are you really like that, or has the author misrepresented you? If you are Dodder in *The Little Grey Man* are you really such a grumpy old devil, or if you are Huck, are you as wicked as people think? Tell about yourself as you really are and how you would like people to think of you.

4. Which of these people in the books would you like to be? Perhaps none of them—why, or why not?

5. Some of the people you have heard about were living unusual lives. Imagine you are a character at some great moment of your own life— it might be great only to you. Read *Over the Bridge*, Chapter 27, by Richard Church (where he gets his first spectacles). Or it might be a great moment in history, for example, the story from Danny Blanchflower's *The Double and before* ... How did it feel to you at that moment in that place?

6. Describe a stranger in:

> an adventure story
> a humorous story
> a fairy story

School

The child's experience of school enters deep and his recollection as an adult is always tinged with feeling, be it distaste, nostalgia, or gratitude. From the age of 5 the school experience is one of the most powerful he has. At school, in classroom or playground, things happen that matter profoundly in the lives of the children. Often we are unaware of their happening or of their importance. If we can help them to share some of these feelings with us creatively, then we shall help them, and ourselves, to come to effective terms with the school experience. The work suggested should lead to a sharper observation and some awareness of others.

This focusing of awareness is one of the primary functions of movement/drama. No worthwhile movement can be achieved until children are aware of the space they are working in and of other people's positions in it. They don't get this facility easily, or by being put on a spot, by girating, or by waving their arms around. They get it by using their eyes. They must be encouraged to regard the space they have as part of themselves and take it with them wherever they go. Certainly in early years before beginning any developed movement work, teachers should give practices aimed at making children space conscious. Some examples of practices are: moving about the hall in different positions with sudden stops to check space; changing directions or speeds on signals; repeated finding and filling of spaces; carrying a 'magic box' which explodes if bodies come too close together. We have also to remember that this sort of work needs constant revision. The **Out of School** movement practices in particular depend a great deal for their success on competent space usage by children. The notes in Part I (p.23) are relevant.

Readings

Willy at School	*A Likely Lad* Ch.7	Gillian Avery
The Unruly Class	*Flood Warning* Ch. 1	Paul Berna
Chancy teaches Indiana the Alphabet	*Chancy and the Grand Rascal* Ch. 13	Sid Fleischman
Esther Goes to School	*The Endless Steppe* Ch. 7	Esther Hautzig

Village School	*Cider with Rosie* Ch. 3	Laurie Lee
Going Home with Miss Olroyd	*No More School* Ch. 1	William Mayne
School Dinners	Anon.	*The Key of the Kingdom* 2
The School Boy	William Blake	*A Flock of Words*
School's Out	W. H. Davies	*Round the Day; Blackwell's Junior Poetry Book* 1; *Poetry and Life* 2; *Rhyme and Rhythm* (red)
School-bell	Eleanor Farjeon	*Round the Day; The Children's Bells*
Numbers	Eleanor Farjeon	*The Children's Bells; Rhyme and Rhythm* (blue)
A History Lesson	Miroslav Holub	*A Flock of Words*
Last Lesson of the Afternoon	D. H. Lawrence	*The Albemarle Book of Modern Verse* 1
Arithmetic	Carl Sandburg	*The Albemarle Book of Modern Verse* 1; *Enjoying Poetry* 2; *Junior Voices* 3; *A Flock of Words; Happenings* 2
Out of School	Hal Summers	*Happenings* 1; *Dawn and Dusk; Enjoying Poetry* 2
'I've got an Apple Ready'	John Walsh	*Round the Day; The Roundabout by the Sea*
Bus to School	John Walsh	*Poetry Panorama* 4; *Rhyme and Rhythm* (yellow); *Mood and Rhythm* 1; *The Roundabout by the Sea; The Key of the Kingdom* 2; *Wordscapes*

Movement/drama

Out of school

Hal Summers' poem contains some fine phrases for movement/drama.

> 'And a bouncing ball'
> 'And a whirling top'
> 'Bully boys reeling off'
> 'Hurt ones squealing off'
> 'Aviators wheeling off'
> 'Mousey ones stealing off'.

Work from these should develop into class drama activities as below:

1. Practise being a bouncing ball. Try to get pattern in your work. Do not be satisfied with just bouncing.
   a. Make a pattern of bounces on the floor.
   b. Alter the height of your bounces. Make this into a pattern, perhaps every third bounce or every bounce in a certain place is big.
   c. Join a. and b. together.
   d. Alter the speed of your bounces. Make a pattern with different speeds.
   e. Try to introduce a really small movement somewhere in your pattern.
   f. Try to introduce a spectacular movement somewhere in your pattern.
   g. Balls also roll. Introduce some rolling into your pattern. Get a good position, both to get into your roll and to get out of it without interrupting the flow of your pattern. Which part of your body is leading the roll? Try to get some other part (say the elbow or the knee) leading the way. Practise your best pattern.
2. Practise whirling like tops. Pay particular attention to:
   a. Speed. Think how a top starts, how it runs down at the finish. The movement might not be continuous or flowing, particularly if the whipper is poor at his job.
   b. The path of movement. Get into a good starting position. Make a pattern on the floor. Try different parts of your body leading the way.
3. Practise whipping a top to make it spin.
   a. Wind the whip on the top carefully.
   b. Start with a quick sudden jerk to get it going.
   c. Remember to alter the speed and frequency of your whipping: fast if it is in danger of falling, slow and less frequent when it is going well.
   d. Work together in pairs at this. One being the whipper, the other the top. Talk it over first to decide what you are going to do, how you are going to start, the path and different speeds you are going to have. The top will need to watch the whipper carefully to respond to his movements. Change over.

4. Practise walking:
    a. As a 'bully boy' would. What else might he do as he walked along,
    Throw something? Kick something? Push someone out of his way?
    Spoil someone's game? Steal something? Fight someone?
    Work out a short sequence of movements and practise it.
    b. As a 'hurt one' would. How does he get hurt? Perhaps he falls, gets
    bumped into or bumps into something. Show clearly which part of
    your body is hurt. Alter this to show other parts involved. Pick out
    the best one and act out your little scene.
    c. As 'mousey ones stealing off'. Move as a very timid person would.
    Think about your head and eyes. See someone or something you
    don't like coming and hide from them or it. Be sure it is gone before
    coming out. Then how are you going to move?

After practice in these activities and others which Hal Summers' and
W.H. Davies' poems will suggest, it should now be possible to build the whole
thing up into a class activity. I would suggest first that:
    a. Children decide what they are going to be.
    b. Points of entry are decided. (There need not be one door: the more
    the better. Similarly all the entrances should not be at the side or
    round the edge).
    c. Times of children coming out are decided. This can be quite arbitrary
    as long as all the tops, bully boys, and so on, do not come out together.
    d. A clear starting signal is given. The ringing of a bell would be ideal.
    e. The children leave the imaginary playground at different times—
    allowing for late comers (possibly showing by their movements why
    they are late), for mothers coming to call their children home, or for
    teachers and caretakers telling them to get off home.
    f. A period of silent calm when it is all ended.
Or second that:
    The teacher or a child could read the poem, making suitable pauses
    between the verses, and the children could play their parts as they
    are mentioned. Again, different points of entry and departure are
    essential: the drama could be ruined if the children are queuing to
    make their entry into the playground through the one specified
    doorway.

Village school
Read again the playground scene on Laurie Lee's first day at school. Be:
    the new boy
    any of the others
    the teacher rescuing the child.

(*Let there be a number of these scenes acted out in groups after the children*

*have had practice in each one. The steps for teaching this scene follow the
same progression as outlined above in* **Out of school**, *with the children
having a wide variety of experience before any large class activity is done.*)

In school

Let's mime some of the things you do at school:

1. *a.* Painting a picture. Stand up and imagine you have a large area to
    paint on and big brushes. Make it as big as you like. Move about your
    picture and look at it from different angles as you work. Mix your
    own paint.
   b. Paint a very small picture with plenty of minute detail.
   c. Do 1. and 2. in slow motion.
   d. Copy a picture from a book. Look carefully at the picture in front
    of you before you begin and keep referring to it from time to time.
   e. Work with a partner. Put him in an interesting position for a picture
    entitled:

    Hands
    Knees
    The Dancer
    Feet

    Get your partner to hold the position while you paint his picture.
    Change over.
    Let the person who has been painted come round and look at the
    finished picture. Then models go round and look at all the other
    pictures.
   f. You are a photographer not a painter. Set up your model again and
    take pictures of him from all angles. Go round the other models,
    taking pictures of them.
2. *a.* Modelling. You have a large lump of clay to model. Get clear in your
    mind what you are going to model and then do so.
   b. Work in pairs through the sequence of 1.*e.* and *f.* applied to modelling.
3. Reading. Sit down and read a book. Try to show from your movements
    what sort of book it is, what you think of it, and if you are going to do
    anything with it.
4. Music. All play the piano, violin, recorder, cymbals, any instrument
    you like.

Written work

1. 'Last Lesson in the Afternoon' expresses a point of view you might not
    appreciate or even have considered. It tells about school in the eyes of a

certain teacher. Do you think your teacher might feel like this? If you were the teacher, what would you find annoying about the day's work?

2. Stories and songs have been written with the idea 'If I were . . .' All right, you *are* the teacher—what would you do? Which things would you keep and which change? Why?

3. Parents are always telling you that 'school has changed since my day' or 'we couldn't have done that'. What do you think your parents' school was like? Which things seem to stick out most in your parents' minds?

4. Write a story 'My first day at school'.

5. How do you feel when you leave school at night? What do you look forward to? Does the next morning loom up at you, or do you feel free? Be honest, for there is the chance that you might miss school when you are not there, and might want to stay at school even in the evenings.

6. Describe the scene in the classroom at the end of the day.

7. Two of the poems ('Out of School' and 'School's Out') are concerned with the coming out of school—peace disturbed by noise. Write about it the other way round, after everyone has gone away. Think of the scene in the playground five minutes before the bell goes and five minutes after: the quiet, some litter left about, the forgotten coat or bag, the departing or gossiping Mums and the late ones catching up with the others. Again you might choose to write this in verse.

8. Tell about school from the caretaker's point of view—'Oh, how I wish these children would . . .'—or you could be the bus conductor, traffic warden at the crossing, or the cook, or any other adult who is concerned with school. What do you think they would wish for from you?

9. Most people have a 'way out' of things they don't like doing or things that don't interest them. All dreaming doesn't take place in bed. What do you do when a lesson gets boring? Tell about it.

10. Make a book about the teachers in the school. You will need to talk to them and ask them questions to make your pen portraits as full as possible. First make a list of the questions you might ask and talk it over with your teacher.

11. Adults say 'school days are the happiest days of your life' (but by then they have usually left). Do you agree with this?

12. Write down the names of two boys and two girls in your school. See if you can put them into a poem.

13. In 'I've got an apple ready' John Walsh tells about a child slightly afraid of the journey to school and the steps she is going to take to avoid the trouble. Have you ever been afraid like this? Tell about it.

Craft activities

1. Design a pattern in bright colours to be chalked on a top.
   (It can be round or square.) Cut it out and put it on something which
   will spin round and see the effect you have created.
2. Make a classroom frieze—'our school'. This can be work in groups, each
   group designing some scenes to show aspects of the work. (*Work should
   be encouraged in other materials in addition to paint and colour to get
   a three dimensional effect.*)
3. Carl Sandburg says some odd things about numbers jumping about. Can
   you make an illustration of this poem? (*The varied illustrations could be
   cut up and mounted to form a composite class picture.*) Try the same
   thing using words, and then colours. (Read *Hailstones and Halibut Bones*
   and *Words, words, words* by Mary O'Neill.)
4. Paint a picture of the things you see, or dream you see, out of the classroom window when a boring lesson is on.
5. Make a playground scene—'Four O'Clock'. It can be abstract if you like.

Work

It is often said that children and young people have the wrong attitude to work these days. I think that children now work harder in real terms than ever before, where school is concerned. However, the interest and motivation they develop at school may well cease to apply when they go out to work as adults. Some aspects of adult work are increasingly alienating and soul-destroying, and it is important that children should have a wider understanding of what work can imply. Through imaginative involvement in the general working experience they may be able to realize the value of work, its potential dignity, and the wonderful sense of achievement it can bring. They will also gain insight into the self-respect and mutual dependence that can be involved in work. The theme lends itself particularly to sensitive observation. The value of direct experience gained by the children visiting factories and other work places, where they are encouraged to observe movements of machines and workers closely, cannot be overstated. From this, mime of an enjoyable and discerning nature will readily arise.

To assist teachers, the poetry readings have been organized under separate headings which can be related to the drama and writing suggestions.

Readings

Navvying	*Peril on the Iron Road* Pt. 2, Ch.2	Bruce Carter
Lily Rose and the Petticoat	*The Family from One End Street* Ch. 2	Eve Garnett
Uncle Podger Hangs a Picture	*Three Men in a Boat* Ch. 3	Jerome K. Jerome
In the Mine	*Weekend in Dinlock*	Clancy Sigal
Starting the Machine	*Saturday Night and Sunday Morning* Ch.1	Alan Sillitoe
Tom Sawyer Whitewashes the Fence	*The Adventures of Tom Sawyer* Ch.2	Mark Twain
Shopkeeping	*Kipps* Ch. 2	H. G. Wells
Making Bullets	*Little House in the Big Woods* Ch. 3	Laura Ingalls Wilder

Machines

The Pigeon	Richard Church	*Mood and Rhythm* 4; *Enjoying Poetry* 4
A Trial Run	Robert Frost	*Selected Poems*
The Guillotine	Wilfrid Gibson	*The Oxford Book of Verse for Juniors* 4
The Secret of the Machines	Rudyard Kipling	*Mood and Rhythm* 4; *Thoughtshapes*
Let Us Be Men	D. H. Lawrence	*Selected Poems*
Steam Shovel	Charles Malam	*Junior Voices* 4
Manual System	Carl Sandburg	*Voices* 2
Portrait of a Machine	Louis Untermeyer	*Mood and Rhythm* 4

Mining

The Collier's Wife	D. H. Lawrence	*Selected Poems*; *Enjoying Poetry* 3
Caliban in the Coalmines	Louis Untermeyer	*Mood and Rhythm* 3; *Enjoying Poetry* 4
The Collier	Vernon Watkins	*Dawn and Dusk*

Farm

Mending Walls	Robert Frost	*Selected Poems*
The Pasture	Robert Frost	*The Oxford Book of Verse for Juniors* 2; *Blackwell's Junior Poetry Book* 3; *Mood and Rhythm* 1; *Selected Poems*
Herding Lambs	Ruth Pitter	*Blackwell's Junior Poetry Book* 4
Sowing	Edward Thomas	*The Oxford Book of Verse for Juniors* 4; *All Day Long*; *Enjoying Poetry* 1
Digging	Edward Thomas	*Voices* 1
Cynddylan on a Tractor	R. S. Thomas	*Happenings* 1; *Dawn and Dusk; Enjoying Poetry* 4
Ploughing in the Mist	Andrew Young	*Collected Poems*

Mill and Factory

A Lone Striker	Robert Frost	*Selected Poems* (verses 2 and 3 for the section about inside the mill)

Girls in a Factory	Denis Glover	*Voices 3*
Factory Windows	Vachel Lindsay	*Rhyme and Reason*

Work

The Things Men have Made	D. H. Lawrence	*Selected Poems*
Wages	D. H. Lawrence	*Every Man Will Shout*
Work	D. H. Lawrence	*Harrap's Junior Book of Modern Verse*
Morning Work	D. H. Lawrence	*Selected Poems*
Man carrying Bale	Harold Monro	*The Oxford Book of Verse for Juniors* 3; *Thoughtshapes*

Songs

Song of the Road Builders	Ewan MacColl	*Rhyme and Rhythm* (yellow)
I'm a Navvy	Traditional	*Voices 2*

No Work

The Idlers	Edmund Blunden	*The Oxford Book of Verse for Juniors* 4; *Poetry Panorama* 4; *The Key of the Kingdom* 2
Leisure	W. H. Davies	*My Kind of Verse*; *The Pilgrim Book of Verse* 2; *The Book of a Thousand Poems*; *Poetry Panorama* 4; *Enjoying Poetry* 5
Toads	Philip Larkin	*Penguin New Poetry*
Will Consider Situation	Ogden Nash	*Every Man Will Shout*
Un	James Reeves	*Rhyme and Rhythm* (blue)
Lazy Man's Song	Arthur Waley (from the Chinese)	*Happenings* 1
Idleness	Andrew Young	*Happenings* 1; *The Albemarle Book of Modern Verse* 1

Movement/drama

Shops

1. Be the assistant in a shop. Decide what sort of shop it is to be before you begin. What sort of things have you to do?

2. Be a customer in a big store going round looking at the goods on sale. Try to show what sort of goods they are by the movements you make and how you look at them. Is the store crowded? This will affect the way you move.
3. Be a demonstrator showing off a new beauty preparation or a new way of stripping wallpaper, or anything else you like. Get your crowd around you and show off your goods. Think of what you are going to say.
4. Some be shop assistants and some shoppers. Work through a scene in a busy store.
5. Go into a clothing shop and try on some garments. They may be hats, coats, shoes, etc. Think of what you are going to do before you begin, and work out a beginning and ending.
6. Work in groups of four—a family of three and a shop assistant. Talk it over to devise a scene where the family comes into the shop and is served.
7. Be a hairdresser in a salon. Welcome a customer and start to work.
8. Be a watchmaker and work at repairing watches. How are you going to move? Think of the care you will have to take.
9. Be a dressmaker or tailor. Work at a suit or frock. Try it on a customer. Examine the fit and mark it for alterations. Sew again.

Building site
1. Going to work.
   a. Drive a car, van, or bicycle to work in heavy traffic, with frequent stops. Make sounds for the way you are travelling.
   b. Walk to work. Are you carrying anything? Get to the site, and prepare for work.
2. Try these different jobs:
   a. Dig trenches.
   b. Lay bricks.
   c. Work with a cement mixer.
   d. Push a wheelbarrow full of cement and tip it.
   e. Carry a hod of bricks up a ladder and along some scaffolding.
   f. Work at laying a tile floor inside a house.
   g. Do some joinery.
   h. Paint some large walls or ceilings.
   i. Paint carefully round a window frame.
   j. Plaster a wall with long smooth sweeps.
   k. Work with a partner at some large job inside a house. Talk it over first to decide what you are going to do and how you are going to move.

  l. Be the architect with your plans and inspect the building that is
     being done. What sort of things will you have to check? Don't forget
     the instruments you might use.
  m. Unload bags of cement from a lorry.
  n. Work with a crane driver and direct the crane down to a pile of timber,
     fasten the load, and direct the crane away. Can you think of anything
     else to do with a partner while operating a crane?
  o. You are all working on a building site. Decide what materials are
     being used, and what stage the building is at. Then decide what jobs
     you are going to do. For some jobs you will need to work in small
     groups, or with partners; some of you might be foremen and see that
     everything is being done; a few might be architects and inspect the
     work.

  (*In all these activities children should be encouraged to make noises
  appropriate to what they are doing.*)

Farming

1. Drive a herd of cows up a lane.
2. Send your sheep dog to bring in the sheep. Think how you are going to
   watch and control him. You might need to help some sheep yourself.
   Herd them down the hill and into your pen, using the dog.
3. Work with a hoe, weeding and chopping up the ground between the rows
   of vegetables.
4. Feed the chickens in the farmyard and collect up the eggs. Feed and
   water various other farm animals: pigs, cows, horses, etc.
5. Clean out the stables or cowshed. What are you going to use? Make your
   washing and sweeping movements big. Put in clean straw.
6. Plant out young seedlings in a row.
7. Repair a fence which has been damaged. Make sure the poles are firm and
   the wire tight. (Read 'Mending Walls' by R. Frost).
8. Pick, trim, and pack lettuces ready for the market.
9. Your fields have been used by picnickers, who have left a great deal of
   litter. See what has heppened, keep your animals away for fear of their
   cutting their hooves, and clean up the mess. Show what you feel about it.
10. Chop down some trees and saw them up into logs.

Office and factory

1. Go through a pile of papers or mail, sorting them into different trays.
   Some might need immediate attention; if so, show what you·will do.
2. Be a typist. Go through the sequence of copy-typing, from putting in the
   paper. Remember to look at what you are copying and bring back the
   carriage on the typewriter.

3. The 'phone rings while you are working. Answer it and show what happens. Try to work out a short scene where you are working at a desk, perhaps typing, perhaps working with books or operating the switchboard, when you are disturbed by a visitor or the telephone, and something happens. Show by your mime what it is.
4. You are working on the assembly line of a large car plant. The cars move slowly along the line by your side and you have to do something. Make the noises of your work.
    a. Have a large 'bolter' in your hands and bolt the doors to the frames as they are swung into position. Pause before the next frame comes along. Then start again.
    b. Fix a wheel on and tighten the nuts that hold it.
    c. Spray underneath the car with anti-rust.
    d. Open the boot, lean in, and fix the rear light wire in place.
    e. Work in groups of about six on an assembly line. Work out a sequence of car shells passing by, and each of you doing something to them. The work will be continuous and co-ordinated.
    f. Inspect the finished cars.
5. Listen again to 'A Lone Striker' and 'Girls in a Factory' and then start to work on a machine of your own. Hear how Arthur began work in *Saturday Night and Sunday Morning*, and then set up a machine for yourself and start to work on it.
6. Try miming these jobs:
       mending shoes
       repairing a car that will not start
       cooking and baking
       scrubbing a floor
       feeding a baby
       bus conducting
       sewing, darning, ironing
       being a pavement artist.

Machines

Throughout this work we are trying to get children to build up patterns of movement of a mechanical nature accompanied by sound. The patterns will be made by children individually and then developed as a part of a group. The sound will be percussion from either the teacher or other children, or sound made by the children themselves, or recorded (e.g. Herb Alpert's 'Spanish Flea', *Listen, Move, and Dance* No.4, H.M.V. CLP 3531). The order of work with sound is a matter of personal choice. Some may prefer to work entirely with children making their own sounds of machines either as individuals or members of a group. This is my preference as it seems to involve the children's imagination more, and has greater possibilities of extension into written English where light and strong 'sound' words can be invented, or selected and arranged.

Generally the points born in mind are:

a. Some practice should be given in body machine shapes. Shapes should be interesting as well as mechanical.

b. The machines will involve cogs, wheels, belts, pulleys, levers, etc. Discussion with the class will determine the kind of machinery they use.

c. Different machine parts move at different speeds.

d. One machine part activates another into a pattern of movement.

e. Constant repetition of movement is needed to give a mechanical quality.

f. Material may be rigid (metal) or pliable (felt, plastic) and this will direct the type of movement.

g. Movements should be made at different heights.

h. Both small and large movements will be used. Discussion will be needed to see which part of the body (eyes, head) is best used for small movements. If the face is not part of the machine, what expression will it have? Some movements may also be continuous.

i. In order to develop full awareness that will enable the child to become a real part of the machine, slow motion work should be introduced frequently. This may take the form of the machine being switched on, and slowly warming up, or the reverse with the machine switching off and running down. We could have a breakdown, or simply a signal for when the machine starts to run in slow motion. This will apply to group or individual work.

Practise some specific machinery movements.

1. Get into a good position to start every time. Think which parts of your body you are going to use and the speed of your movement at different times. Practise each one several times. Explore fully the movements of:

   a. A 'boring' machine.

   b. A machine with a twisting action.

   c. A heavy, slow, strong machine.

   d. Office machinery, with action that is rapid, jerky, and light. Listen to a typewriter working, with its clicking, clattering, ringing, and sweeping noises. Make the noises yourself. Move to other equipment (e.g. duplicator).

   e. A heavy stamping or pressing machine. Use different parts of your body for the press. Let there be a distinct 'press'.

   f. A machine which sparks and splutters.

   g. A folding machine.

2. Get into a machine position. Listen to these rolling and clanging sounds (*drum, cymbal*). Make up a movement to fit this sound. Carry on making

a pattern of your movements each time the sound is repeated. Think of your path through the air or on the ground.

Listen to another sound. (*It doesn't matter what this is, it could be hissing, grinding, tapping with wooden sticks. The aim is to develop the movements just practised to build up a more complex pattern.*) Move one part of your machine to this sound. Practise until you are sure of your best movement.

Go back to the rolling and the clanging. Start with that, and when you hear the new sound, add your new movement. Repeat the machine movements as the sounds occur in a regular pattern. There may be movements when there is no sound.

Work with a partner. One of you is going to respond to the first sound pattern and one to the second. Talk it over so that your movements follow each other, and work through your sequence when the sounds occur.

A third sound pattern and its movements might well be added to the existing movements and worked into your sequence when the sounds occur.

3. Now you are going to make sounds of your own. Shut your eyes and hear the whirring, clanging, hissing, banging, grinding of machines. Pick out just one or two of these sounds and listen to them by themselves. Say them to yourself until you are sure of them. From your starting position, invent a movement to fit your sound. Repeat the sound over and over again, bringing different parts of your body into the movement each time. Work at this until you have a machine sequence of three or four movements with sounds which can be repeated. Try to vary the strength of the sound and movement, and remember the speed and height you are working at.

Work with a partner at your first sound and movement. One part of the machine is going to move the other. Discuss the sounds you are each going to make before you begin. Enlarge the group to four or so, each making a sound and movement in a pattern. Now you might have to do something in response to each other's sounds and will have movements of many kinds, some of them continuous.

While this is going on, a bang on the cymbal indicates that the machine breaks down. Discuss one part failing, what sound it is going to make, and what happens to the other parts. Show what happens.

Add another person to your group. He is going to be the machine operator. What is his role? Let him start the machine in some way and work with it, perhaps feeding it, taking and moving things, and so on.

Let the machine break down while he is there. What is he going to do now? Prepare for the machine getting out of control. Let the speed of your pattern begin to vary. Have the machine working at normal speed, then running slowly, irregularly, and running out of control, then exploding (*provide a signal first*). Think how the different parts of the machine will react, some spasmodic, some grinding, some twisted. Be sure of your finishing position.

Coal mining
Read *Weekend in Dinlock* (p.165 onwards) first.
1. Shut your eyes and see the road and coal face. Can you hear the men working? When you are sure of what the paths are like, move as you would down a pit road. Clamber over rough rocks and pieces of coal that jut out. Move in different positions as the conditions make you.
2. Get in a position to watch the men at work on the coal face. Think of the smell, the air, the dust, and how you will use your lamp.
3. Help a man who is building and packing the buttresses, smoothing out the roof, and putting in the props.
4. Go to work with a pick on the coal face as the men do. Remember your working position. Pick in short sharp bursts and wrench the coal away with force. What happens when it falls? Work out a sequence of movements with work, rests, and drinks. Sometimes your work will be slowed down by the hardness of the rock you're cutting through. You might need to alter your position from time to time. Practise working as though you were a skilled miner; a visitor having a first try. How will your movements differ in these two situations? Try working on your side like the man in the small crypt.
5. Now try shovelling coal on to the conveyor belt, again with pauses, bursts of work, and shifts of position.
   Can you arrange your work in a pattern like the men did? Some worked smoothly and regularly, others in bursts, some hummed a song to themselves. Choose the way of working which would suit you best over a long period of time.
6. Work with a partner. One to do the picking, the other the shovelling. Try to work as a team and respond to each other.
7. Get into groups of six or eight. Talk over all the jobs that were going on at the coal face. Decide what you are going to do and work through a group sequence with as many operations going on at the same time as possible. Change over to do some other job.
   Work now as a gang coming through the paths to the coal face, getting

ready for work, breaking off to rest, and continuing work. Think of all the things you will have to do.

8. When you are working you hear the rumble of a fall of rock (*percussion signal*). Show what you do. Is it near or far away? One of your mates in the gang is hurt. Talk it over first to decide what happens. Then help him away.

9. Work out a mime called 'Disaster at the Pit'.

Written work

1. Think of the machinery, noise, smell, and appearance inside a mill or factory. Write about it.

2. From your movement on machines, explain your machine and how it works.

3. Write about the operator and the day at the factory when his machine went out of control.

4. Would you rather work in the town or in the country? What advantage has each got?

5. Do you like going to the shops with your parents? What is it like in a busy store when you are taken there?

6. Write a poem entitled 'Machines'. Use the sound words you invented when you were a machine.

7. You are a mischievous child. You go into a factory and push a button which starts the machinery. Tell what happens.

8. Have you ever seen a person doing a job they were very good at, and noticed the ease and confidence of their movements? Tell about it.

9. Would you like to spend your days in idleness? How often do you ask 'What can I do?' when on holiday, and get an unsatisfactory answer? Tell what happens to you.

10. Make up a work song for some jobs (e.g. mending shoes, getting the baby to feed or to sleep, pushing a barrow, painting).

11. Have you ever been in trouble for not doing a job properly? Tell about it, particularly why you didn't do it well—or perhaps why you did!

12. What is it like in your district when the factories close? 'The hooter sounds and . . .'

13. Some people make hard work of a little job, like Uncle Podger did. Make up a story of your own, where a small job grows to involve many people and ends in disaster of a humorous kind.

14. You are someone else walking down the street to work. You may be a coalman, dustman, shop assistant, teacher, factory worker, or any person

you wish. What are you thinking? Tell how you feel going to work and how you look forward to the coming day.

15. You are looking through a window watching people at work as we heard in 'A Lone Striker'. What would you see and how would you feel? You might be a visitor to this planet from space. Describe what you saw as an onlooker.

16. Most children like to help adults at work. Have you ever helped one of these people: builders, farmers, shopkeepers, teachers, van drivers? Tell what happened.

17. In R.S. Thomas' poem, Cynddylan grew when he was on his tractor. He took great pride in his job. What do you do better than anyone else, the job at which you know you are the master? Tell what it is and what it means to you.

18. Have you ever started a job to help someone, and finished up in an awful mess as Lily Rose did? Tell about it and how you felt. You might like to title it 'I remember'.

Reading for younger children

Very often with younger children the topic 'People who work for us' is taken. Opportunities for movement/drama and writing that involve insight and identification are often not fully exploited. The following list may help teachers working with younger children who would like to incorporate mime and drama based on this theme and extend it into writing.

Casey Jones	Anon.	*The Oxford Book of Verse for Juniors* 4; *Mood and Rhythm* 2; *Pegasus* 2; *The Oxford Book of Poetry for Children*
The Vet	Guy Boas	*The Pattern of Poetry*
Snobs	Richard Church	*Mood and Rhythm* 4
The Barber's	Walter de la Mare	*Exploring Poetry* 2
The Busman	Eleanor Farjeon	*Blackwell's Junior Poetry Book* 1
Mr. Coggs	E. V. Lucas	*Blackwell's Junior Poetry Book* 3; *Exploring Poetry* 2; *The Book of a Thousand Poems*
The Postman	Clive Sansom	*The Book of a Thousand Poems*

The Dustman	Clive Sansom	*Blackwell's Junior Poetry Book* 1
The Policeman	Clive Sansom	*Blackwell's Junior Poetry Book* 1
The Lighthouse Keeper	R. L. Stevenson	*The Oxford Book of Verse for Juniors* 4

Rooms

In this theme the cultivation of the senses of seeing, hearing, touching, and smelling is vitally important if the standard of work is to be high. Reference should be made to the section on sense training in Part I (p.17).

In the movement/drama section I have listed some exercises designed to develop concentration and to bring out the sensory possibilities inherent in this theme. They can, of course, be used elsewhere, as indicated in Part I, p.24.

Readings

The Caves in the Cliff	*On the Run* Ch.15	Nina Bawden
The Entrance Hall	*The Children of Green Knowe*	Lucy M. Boston
The Tots in the Tower	*The Wheel on the School* Ch.14	Meindert De Jong
David's New Bedroom	*David Copperfield* Ch.3	Charles Dickens
The Unused Room	*Great Expectations* Ch. 8	Charles Dickens
The Cellar	*The Four Storey Mistake* Ch. 3	Elizabeth Enright
Into the Secret Room	*The Four Storey Mistake* Ch. 6	Elizabeth Enright
Mr Badger's House	*The Wind in the Willows* Ch. 4	Kenneth Grahame
Mole's House	*The Wind in the Willows* Ch. 5	Kenneth Grahame
Solomon's Treasure Chamber	*King Solomon's Mines* Ch. 17	Sir H. Rider Haggard
Totto's Laboratory	*The Hungry Cloud* Ch. 4	Tom Ingram
Stig's Cave	*Stig of the Dump* Ch.1	Clive King.
The Kitchen	*Cider With Rosie* Ch.4	Laurie Lee

Mr. Timm's Cave	*The Lion, the Witch, and the Wardrobe* Ch.2	C. S. Lewis
The Smuggler's Hut	*Jim Davis* Ch. 8	John Masefield
Holiday Memory	*Quite Early One Morning*	Dylan Thomas
Merlin's House	*The Sword in the Stone* Ch. 3	T.H. White

Country Bedroom	Frances Cornford	*Harrap's Junior Book of Modern Verse*
Bickers Cottage	Frances Cornford	*The Oxford Book of Verse for Juniors* 4
Cottage	Eleanor Farjeon	*A Puffin Quartet of Poets*
My Hut	E. Mathias	*The Book of a Thousand Poems*
The Doll House	Phyllis McGinley	*Round the Day*
The Barn	Stephen Spender	*The Harrap Book of Modern Verse*
The Hayloft	R. L. Stevenson	*Poetry and Life* 2
The Seed Shop	Muriel Stuart	*The World Around*; *The Pattern of Poetry*

Movement/drama

1. Close your eyes. Listen to all the sounds you can hear. Try to think how many there are. Listen to one of those sounds until you can hear just that one. Listen to yourself breathing. Can you hear someone else breathing? Try to concentrate on another sound, then go back to hearing yourself breathe.
2. Look at the floor, just one section or floorboard. Feel it and look at it until you know exactly what it is like. Is it different from the next section or piece of wood? How?
3. Look at the wall. Is it all one colour or pattern? How many shades of colour can you really see?
4. You have a pile of fine sand in front of you. Close your eyes and let it run through your fingers; lift it up by handfuls and let it fall down.
5. Close your eyes and stroke a cat's fur, a dog, a piece of cloth, a snake. Have you ever felt you must touch something? What was it like? See it, and then touch and feel it. Why do cats rub against people's legs? Give something the lightest touch you can. Move around touching things lightly, stroking things.

6. Look at your hand. Examine it so that you know everything about it, both back and front. Is it different from someone else's hand you know? How?

7. Reach out with your foot to feel something. Decide what it is you are to feel first:

> test the water with your toe
> stroke something with your foot
> walk barefooted over a pebbly beach
> someone is stroking a feather over your foot; can you feel it?

8. Close your eyes and move around trying to sense other people and avoid them.

9. Close your eyes. Can you smell

> wet clothes drying
> salt and vinegar
> burning wood
> any fruit
> petrol
> the dining room.

(Read parts of 'Quite Early One Morning' by Dylan Thomas, which gives a good impression of sensory awareness by a writer.)

10. Look round the room in which you are sitting. You are going to be able to alter it to make it into a club, coffee bar, or whatever you wish. Get clear in your mind's eye what you would like to do; the type of decorations, room dividers, and so on, that you would have, and how the room would be laid out.

11. Work with a partner and explain to each other the things you have decided you would do.

12. Show by movements how you would feel on going into these rooms you have created and how you would behave in them.

Develop this to show what would happen once you are in:

a. A dentist's surgery.

b. The Hall of Mirrors at a fun fair.

c. An old attic room in a disused house. Perhaps this has not been entered for years and years and is filled with junk which you can examine and play with.

d. A waiting room where all the seats are taken.

e. A cave in which you suspect someone is hiding.

f. A strange room at night without a light.

g. The smoke-filled bedroom of a house on fire. How are you going to get in? Is the floor, roof, or any other part in danger of falling?

Develop this into a short scene where you hear someone call from a blazing house, enter it, find them, and get them out.

   h. The control room in a nuclear reactor station. You have to watch and work the switches, dials, and machines.

13. Be like Stig and make your room in the old tip. Think how you will move all the things you want to use.

14. Work with a partner. Try to show your partner by movement that you are entering, or are in, a particular room. Show him how you feel about it. Let him try to guess what room it is and talk it over. Change places.

15.*a.* Which shop do you like going into? Think about all the things to look at when you go in and how you examine them. Go round the shop looking at things.

   b. Imagine you are:

      a parent buying clothes for a child

      a person 'browsing' round a bookshop

      shopping in a very busy supermarket

      choosing something in a very expensive shop.

   c. Be the person working in any shop you like. You could be:

      a hairdresser

      a dressmaker or tailor fitting someone

      a model showing expensive clothes

      a studio photographer taking a family photograph. Arrange your group several times until you are satisfied with their position. Look at it from all angles; make sure your lighting is right before you take the photograph.

16. Let's all go into the same room, say a large gymnasium with all the equipment you could wish for—bars, boxes, trampolines, weights, punch balls, rolling mats, Indian clubs, chest stretchers, stomach narrowers. Close your eyes and see the place. As soon as you have decided what you are doing, move off and start. Change over to use some other piece of equipment.

Written work

1. Describe a room in your own house. (Listen again to the description of Laurie Lee's kitchen).

2. You are in a witch's or wizard's cave or room. Tell what it is like. Think about the light, the smell, and the unusual things that might be there.

3. See a room, which is familiar to you, as a strange animal or person would. Tell about it as they would see it.

4. Write about the bedroom you would like to have.
5. What would you do to improve your classroom? Write about what you would like to be like.
6. Which is your favourite room, the one you feel best in? Why?
7. Have you ever been in an unusual room, in an old castle perhaps, or a farmhouse? Tell about it.
8. Have you ever had to stay in bed while you were sick? Did you notice anything then about your room that you had not noticed before or imagine it was anything else? What did you play at? If you have not been sick, then make a list of all the things you would do to your room to make it fit for a child who has to stay in it for a while.
9. Write about Merlin's house or Mr. Timm's cave as though you had been there.
10. Write a description of a church, cinema, or large shop. Try to impart the particular atmosphere of the place and how it makes you feel.

Storms

As a source of fantasy the extreme elements of weather are highly evocative, seeming to stir the primeval feelings reflected in much of our folklore. Opportunities for the exploitation of direct experience are perhaps limited, but if they occur, should be taken up to the full. Pieces written during, or immediately after, a storm could be expected to be vital and personal, particularly if the teacher is ready with appropriate material. The example given by Sybil Marshall in *An Experiment in Education*, Chapter 5, is well worth reading.

Indirect experience, however, is also available, since contemporary reporting of storms is common. The plight of trawlermen in Arctic storms, the breaking up of a ship on the rocks with a resultant oil slick, or the troubles of a storm-bound adventurer provide ready material for our children's imaginations and an avenue for identification.

Readings

The Great Storm	*The Oxford Book of Stories for Juniors*	(ed.) James Britton (story by Francis Kilvert)
Prairie Storm	*The Custer Wolf* Ch. 9	Roger Caras
The Storks in the Storm	*The Wheel on the School* Ch.11	Meindert De Jong
The Storm in the Treehouse	*The Four Storey Mistake* Ch. 5	Elizabeth Enright
Mountain Storms	*Annapurna* Ch. 12, 14	Maurice Herzog
Tropical Storm	*A High Wind in Jamaica* Ch.1	Richard Hughes
Riding through the Storm	*Snow Cloud, Stallion* Ch. 12	Gerald Raftery
The Storm	*The Silver Sword* Ch. 27	Ian Serraillier
The Storm	*Hills End* Ch.5	Ivan Southall
The Snowstorm	*Children on the Oregon Trail* Ch.10	A. Rutgers van der Loeff

October Blizzard	*The Long Winter* Ch. 4	Laura Ingalls Wilder
Praise Song of the Wind	Anon.	*Junior Voices* 2
Storms	Glynis Burr	*Junior Voices* 3
From 'Snow Storm'	John Clare	*A Flock of Words*
The Storm	Emily Dickinson	*The Oxford Book of Verse for Juniors* 3; *My Kind of Verse*
Storm Fear	Robert Frost	*Selected Poems*
Wind	Ted Hughes	*A Flock of Words*; *Junior Voices* 4
A Storm in Childhood	T. H. Jones	*A Flock of Words*
Thunder and Lightning	James Kirkup	*Pegasus* 2
Thunder	Walter de la Mare	*Iron, Honey, Gold* 1
Electric Storm	Michael C. Martin	*The Albemarle Book of Modern Verse* 1
Glass Falling	Louis MacNeice	*The Oxford Book of Verse for Juniors* 4
Giant Thunder	James Reeves	*The Pattern of Poetry*; *My Kind of Verse*
From 'Stormy Day'	W. R. Rodgers	*All Day Long*
Storm-wind	Christina Rossetti	*The Oxford Book of Verse for Juniors* 2
The Storm	Ian Serraillier	*The Ballad of Kon-Tiki, and other verses*
	Ian Serraillier	*Everest Climbed*
The Storm	Edward Shanks	*Poetry Panorama* 3; *Exploring Poetry* 4; *All Day Long*
After the Storm	William Wordsworth	*Poetry and Life* 4; *The Oxford Book of Verse for Juniors* 4; *Rhyme and Rhythm* (yellow)

Movement/drama

General

1. You are in a great storm. Show yourself:
> walking
> sheltering, then going on

searching for someone
manning the wheel of a boat
trying to put up an umbrella
keeping a lookout
closing house doors and putting up shutters
being lost
being trees in the wind (think of your body shape and which
parts move).

2. Make a pattern of storm movements with your body.

   a. Make a sound like the wind. Alter the pitch and strength of your
   sound at different times. Move to match your wind sounds.
   Think how you are going to alter the speed of your movements and
   the position you will be in when still.

   b. Listen to the roll and crash of the cymbal. What does this sound like
   (*thunder*)? Practise making thunder-like movements when you hear
   the cymbal. Sometimes they will be sudden, sharp movements and
   at other times rumblings leading to a crash. (*Give varied experience
   by altering cymbal and tambour noises.*)

   c. Go back to your own wind noises and movements. Practise them
   again to make sure you know what you are doing. When you hear
   the thunder noises, add the thunder movements. Listen carefully to
   the sound the cymbal makes and, when it is finished, continue as
   the wind.
   Now make your own thunder noise. Practise it first; you might find
   it better to shut your eyes before you begin and think of the sort of
   sounds you are going to try to make. Make movements to fit in with
   your sounds—sudden claps, low rumbles, murmurs, and so on. Add
   your own thunder noises and movements to the wind noises and
   movements you have already made.

   d. How does lightning move? Try to move your hands and arms like
   lightning. Bring your body into it to alter the height and path of your
   lightning. How many paths are you taking? Make other parts of your
   body lead the movement.
   Make a lightning sound. Practise it until you have a good crackling
   sound. Make your movements fit the sound.

   e. Go back to your wind and sound movements and now put in your
   crackling sound and lightning movements.
   Can you work out a storm scene yourself, moving as the wind, thunder,
   and lightning? Work on your own to get all the sounds and movements
   into a pattern to make up a storm scene by yourself.

  f. Do it now as a class. Some be the wind, some the thunder, and
  some the lightning. (*Arrange signals for the children to start on.*)
  When you get very good, you will be able to work without the signals
  by listening and responding to the other children.

Giant thunder

1. Shut your eyes and hear a giant saying the words 'Hag wife, hag wife,
   bring me my bones'. Practise hearing, then saying these lines in as many
   ways as you can, putting the emphasis on different words. Remember
   it might not all be strong or angry. He could be a timid giant.
   Move as your giant would when saying the words. Try as many different
   ways as you can of matching your movements to different ways of
   speaking. Go round to watch and listen to the way other children are
   speaking and moving.
   Pick out your best way of speaking and moving, and practise that until
   you are sure of it.
2. Now try the same exercises for the hag, saying 'They are not done'
   sorrowfully, angrily, fearfully, etc. Again practise different ways of
   moving and speaking, with your movements matching the way you are
   speaking.
3. Some be giants and some hags. The hags take up a position while the
   giants stride home. What might the hag be doing? Remember your body
   shapes.
   Will the hag hear the giant approaching? If so, how will she react, knowing the bones are not done? Be doing something, and, when the giants
   speak their lines, react to them and respond with your own lines. (*This
   is quite individual work. A signal for the giants to start speaking might
   help, but they should not speak in chorus, or move, or finish simul-
   taneously.*)
   Change over your parts and practise again. Do it several times to try all
   possibilities of both giant and hag.
   Work with a partner. Talk over what sort of characters you are going to
   be, and respond to each other as you work through the scene.
4. Try to add some more dialogue between the giant and the hag before he
   starts to overturn the pot, so that it develops into a quarrel between
   them. Perhaps the hag nags, or storms away leaving the giant, in which
   case he will have to act differently. Talk it over first and see how your
   dialogue develops.
   You might wish to write it out later, coming to a different ending, then
   you can act this new story through.
   Add other characters: children, relatives, or neighbours listening to the
   quarrel.

5. Take the verse 'All the world ... creature wakes'. Practise being:
   a. The thunder as in **General**. (*Alter length of rolls preceding crash*.)
   b. Forest and trees shaking. Make your own sounds for this on teacher's signal.
   c. Living creatures waking. Listen to giant thunder approaching as the drum beats. Think how they would wake, listen, react, and move. Develop this into reacting to sound patterns as for thunder in **General** 2.b. Be as many creatures as you can and react as they become involved. Sometimes you will be moving, at other times still.
6. Practise being the giant saying the words 'I'll have them, cooked or not' all the ways you can. Move to fit the ways of speaking as you did in 1. and 2. above.
7. Work as a class. Let's have some giants, some hags, mountains, forests, thunder, wind, creatures, and rainstorms. All do your own part and work to the percussion signals you have been given before. On the signal, giants and hags speak out your lines as you have practised them, and everyone react all the time.
8. Work in groups of about ten. You have had practice in the early part of the story. Can you work out an ending? Talk it over and when you have decided on an ending, work through your group scene based on the poem. Add more characters, change and alter the plot if you wish. Change over parts until you get the result you like best.

Kon Tiki
Be the men:
   a. Sleeping where they tumbled and being disturbed by the storm.
   b. Clinging for dear life to the steering wheel two at a time.
   c. Hailing the passing ship.
   d. Lashing the cargo; bailing out.
   e. Furling the sail.
Work with particular parts of the body emphasized: eyes, mouth, and face. Feel the wind and spray. Your hands are in different positions; your legs and body must change their stance to withstand the storm.

The practices should be interwoven so that eventually several things are going on at the same time, with all the children involved either as groups or individuals, with the usual principles of varying the parts. The children may now be ready to plan out in groups the scene of the Kon Tiki in the storm. They must have plenty of opportunity to read the extract, talk it over, and perhaps write out the sequence of events they are to follow, with additions to characters, and plot if they so desire. Storm music (e.g. Overture: Fingal's Cave *by Mendelssohn*) will provide a key background for

much of what happens. There is also a special place here for the development of a dialogue between the characters. This will need practice. The
points to consider are the building of a vocabulary to express the situation,
and the development of a flexible range of vocal tone to suit different
situations which will occur.

Camping

You are asleep in a tent and are awakened by the sound of an approaching
storm. Show how you would react and what you would do.

   a. Wake up and listen.

   b. Feel the rain creeping up under the groundsheets.

   c. Hold the tent pole as it strains.

   d. Go out to slacken the ropes.

   e. Try to take down the tent.

   Work in groups of four to develop a mime based on a storm while you
were camping out. Think carefully about the progression of events and
particularly the ending.

Written work

1. Tell the story of a storm.
2. Have you ever had to reassure your younger brother or sister during
   thunder or lightning? What happened? How did you feel and what did
   you do?
3. You are awakened in the night by the sound of thunder and the flashing
   of lightning. Shut your eyes, see what happens, then write the story.
   Tell your feelings honestly.
4. Can you shape a piece of writing so that it looks like a storm? You
   might need to break up words and re-arrange them.
5. If you have ever been out in a boat when the sea grew rough, write about
   what it felt like to you.
6. Listen again to the readings about mountain storms, and then write
   about what you think it would be like in such a storm.
7. Think of a fairly easy job and describe doing it in the difficulties of a
   storm.
8. Thor heard voices when he was in difficulties and danger. Has this ever
   happened to you? Read the passage again and try to tell what he was
   thinking. How do you think the crew of the Kon Tiki felt?
9. Tell the story of the ride through the storm. Have you ever been on a
   journey in a storm such as the one in *Snow cloud, Stallion*? What was
   it like?

Night

This theme involves both fantasy and sensory experience. There can be no doubt about the role fantasy plays in children's lives and here it is identified with everyday things like coming home, going to bed, and the darkness of night.

Darkness obviously leads to exploration through the senses of touch and smell, and the theme is a good area for the general development of concentration. The practice in remaining perfectly still on a signal is a most useful concentration exercise applicable to other movement activities. (See Part I, p.24.)

Readings

Night on the Marsh	*Journey from Peppermint Street* Ch.8	Meindert De Jong
Thoughts in a Strange Bed	*Great Expectations* Ch.45	Charles Dickens
The Town at Night	*The Key* Ch.14	Eilís Dillon
Flying to the Midnight Feast	*The Summer Birds* Ch. 6	Penelope Farmer
Out at Night	*Jack Holborn* Ch. 5	Leon Garfield
Kai in Bed	*The Hungry Cloud* Ch. 7	Tom Ingram
Ranofer out at Night	*The Golden Goblet* Ch. 11	E. J. McGraw
In the Tent	*The Fox Hole* Ch. 4	Ivan Southall
In the Dead of the Night	*Growing Summer* Ch. 23	Noel Streatfield
Hugh Escapes at Night	*Brother Dusty-Feet* Ch. 1	Rosemary Sutcliff
Tom and Huck in the Graveyard	*The Adventures of Tom Sawyer* Ch. 9	Mark Twain

Night	William Blake	*Come Hither; Exploring Poetry* 4; *Birthright Poetry* 1; *The Book of a Thousand Poems; The Merry-Go-Round*
A Strange Meeting	W. H. Davies	*Common Ground; Mood and Rhythm* 4; *The Oxford Book of Poetry for Children*
Prelude	T. S. Eliot	*Dawn and Dusk; Common Ground; Flash Point*
The Night Will Never Stay	Eleanor Farjeon	*Come Hither; The Oxford Book of Verse for Juniors* 1; *Silver-Sand and Snow; Poetry Panorama* 3; *Poetry and Life* 3
Autumn	T. E. Hulme	*Flash Point; My Kind of Verse; The Faber Book of Children's Verse*
Above the Dock	T. E. Hulme	*Flash Point*
Thief in the Night	D. H. Lawrence	*Voices* 1
Noises in the Night	Thomas Middleton	*The Oxford Book of Verse for Juniors* 1
Sounds in the Night	Coventry Patmore	*Blackwell's Junior Poetry Book* 4
The Moonlight Tree	Dennis Pitt	*Every Man Will Shout*
These marvels were the days, what words can paint the night ...	Ian Serraillier	*The Ballad of Kon-Tiki, and other verses*
Check	James Stephens	*Exploring Poetry* 4; *The Oxford Book of Verse for Juniors* 1; *Poetry and Life* 3; *Blackwell's Junior Poetry Book* 2; *Birthright Poetry* 4; *Poetry Panorama* 4; *The Book of a Thousand Poems*

Movement/drama

Sensory practices

1. Sit on the floor. Feel its hardness on your bottom. Feel it with your fingers. Feel it with some other part of your body. With your fingers try to press the floor down a hundredth of an inch. Try with some other part of your body.

   Can you think of some words to describe the floor as you sit on it? Now lie down and feel the hardness on your body. It changes into a soft bed. Feel it change and react to it now. You have a hot water bottle. Feel the warm part of your bed. Move the bottle to get other parts warm.

2. Work with a partner.

   Blindfold your partner. Is night as dark as this? Tell your partner how you feel in the darkness. Your partner is going to touch you with different things (feathers, spikes, brushes, etc.). Try to tell him what he has used and what it feels like.

   Move about blindfolded. If you come to something, stop, and explore it. When you finish, tell your partner what your movements were like. What about your breathing?

3. You are in bed. Listen to the noises. Can you hear a dripping tap, a rustling curtain, scratching noises? How do they affect you? Listen to just one of them. Make noises yourself like those you hear at night time. Practise different noises.

   Work with a partner. One of you make a noise, the other be in bed reacting to it. You might have to make your noise a few times before you get a response. Repeat the noise at intervals until the sleeper has to get up to investigate it. How will the sleeper move then and what is going to happen? (*Ask the children to listen in bed at home to the noises they hear and recall one of them the next day.*)

4. Be in a tent at night. Hear the creaking and flapping of the canvas and ropes. Get up, feel for your shoes, and, without disturbing any of the others in your tent, go out and fix a loose rope.

5. Move as you would in the dark at night:
   a. In an old graveyard. Try this alone, and with a partner.
   b. In a badly lit district looking for a particular house in a street.
   c. In a junkyard.
   d. Feeling your way along a wall.
   e. Through a wood. Think of the sounds you might hear, the shapes you might see, and how they would effect you.
   f. Running away from someone over uneven ground. You come to a chasm, you can't see the other side. Try to feel for it with various

parts of your body. You are going to have to make a jump in the dark. Think how you are going to feel before you begin. When you are ready, make your jump and continue on your way.

g. Trying to find your seat in a darkened cinema.

h. Along the top of a narrow wall.

In a strange room

Feel around for the doorway.

Move into the room, then about it, feeling your way. What happens when you bump into something?

Practise entering a strange room in the dark and moving about searching for something. Do you make any sounds?

Come across an old chest. Examine it in the dark, find the lock, and open the chest. Reach in. What sort of things could happen now?

Talk it over with a partner to decide what might be in the chest, then show how the different things affect you.

Act through the scene where Ranofer goes into his brother's room. (*The Golden Goblet*, end of Chapter 10)

Getting out at night

Tiptoe from the room as though you were trying to get out without being heard. Try it again carrying something. How are you going to react to a loose floor-board, coughing in the next room or next bed, a squeaking door? A signal from the teacher means that you have made a noise. 'Freeze' when you hear it. Come out of your freeze in your own time and continue. Go downstairs without making a sound. You will need to test every stair before putting your weight on it. Come to a locked and bolted door and open it without making a noise. Feel your way along a dark passage. What will you do if you bump into something by accident?

Hear someone coming and hide from them. They must not see you. When it is safe, carry on along the dark passage.

Work with a partner on getting out at night. One can be out to begin with. He will need to signal, watch out for the other, and help him. Talk it over first to decide whay you are going to do. (Read *The Adventures of Tom Sawyer*, Chapter 9.)

Out at night

1. Be a policeman on night duty. Go around testing doors, shining your torch in windows, etc. What other things can you add to this?

2. Be a sentry on night duty. You hear a sound and go to investigate.

3. Be a watchman with a dog. Work out a scene where something happens.

4. Go tracking at night, following footprints, signs, etc. Remember you will have to look and listen.

5. Follow someone. Take up a position for watching them first. Show what happens as you get colder, your feet get wet, a dog comes sniffing at you. Your quarry moves off and you follow. You lose him in a dark alley. What are you going to do? How are you going to move down the alley?

6. Something frightens or attacks you. What might it be?
   Talk it over first to decide what is going to happen, before you act through this section. Show clearly what happens. Try to end your story by reaching your safely lit room.

7. Creep up to some others in a dark place to try to hear what they are saying (read *Jack Holborn*).
   Work with a partner so that the two of you get into a position to listen to other people. How are you going to react to what they say and keep in touch with each other? (*The Adventures of Huckleberry Finn*, or *Jack Holborn*.) Add a group of men to this scene.
   Let them gather to plot in the dark while the others creep up and listen. Try to get a scene where you can react to each other.

Written work

1. Write a poem 'Night', 'Shadows', or 'Darkness'.
2. Does your mother ever leave the light outside your room on when you are in bed? What does it seem like?
3. Tell about any time you have been out in the dark.
4. Write about the lights you see at night.
5. Describe the noises you sometimes hear when you are lying awake in bed.
6. Have you ever been unable to go to sleep? Tell what it was like.
7. Tell about any of the things you did in the strange room.
8. Write a story 'My Jump in the Dark'.
9. In *The Golden Goblet* when he was afraid of a dark place Ranofer said a charm. What do you do to give yourself confidence?
10. On holidays or at other times you might sleep in strange beds. Tell about your first night in a strange bed.
11. Have you ever hidden in a dark place? What was it like? Tell about it.
12. Tell the story of your night in the graveyard as though you were Tom or Huck.

Bonfires and Fireworks

This is obviously a seasonal theme and one of shorter duration than the others. Not so short though, as children are occupied with this for a long time before the fire is lit, and for many it is a justifiable excuse for raiding, begging, getting dirty, fighting, guarding, eating, burning clothes, and staying up late, which has few rivals during the year. To younger children, the only equal as a source of wonder and excitement is Christmas Eve. The few days after the bonfire can also provide fruitful experience.

As a field of sensory experience it is particularly valuable and much of the work on sounds and smells included in **Rooms** is applicable, and can be extended. The greatest impact will be made if the experiences are directed towards one particular thing. The difference between children writing generally about their bonfires or fireworks after the great day, and what we are looking for, is that here the teacher knows which aspect of the experience she wants the children to explore fully, and isolates elements of that for study in depth. She does not know the responses and must not try to direct those.

The best results in movement/drama will be obtained if the work is first done without mentioning fireworks. Then the children will develop a movement vocabulary which they can later apply to the specific situation. The teacher should know what sort of movement experience she is aiming at and direct towards this, giving experience in explosions, soft flowing movements, rockets, and zig-zags before these are pointed out as fireworks.

In view of the amount of important publicity given lately to the dangers of fireworks and bonfires, many teachers will feel that this aspect should be the one to be isolated and dwelt on in depth.

Readings

The Bonfire	*A Handful of Thieves* Ch 5.	Nina Bawden
The Bonfire	*The Ghost Downstairs* Ch. 3	Leon Garfield
The Bonfire	*Plot Night* Ch. 17	William Mayne

Bonfire Night	Dylan Thomas	*Quite Early One Morning*
The Fifth of November	Anon.	*The Merry-Go-Round*
Anagram for Guy Fawkes Night	Frances Cornford	*The Key of the Kingdom* 3
'Please to Remember'	Walter de la Mare	*Blackwell's Junior Poetry Book* 1; *The Oxford Book of Verse for Juniors* 2; *Poetry and Life* 2; *Poetry Panorama* 2
The Guy	Robert L. Holmes	*Every Man Will Shout*
Fireworks	James Reeves	*A Puffin Quartet of Poets; Poetry and Life* 2; *Blackwell's Junior Poetry Book* 3; *Enjoying Poetry* 1
Fireworks	Phyllis Reid	*Round the Year*
Gunpowder Plot	Vernon Scannell	*The Albemarle Book of Modern Verse* 1; *Voices* 2; *Flash Point*; *A Flock of Words*
Firework Night	Eric Simpson	*Every Man Will Shout*

Movement/drama

Fireworks

1. Practise jumping up and down. As you jump, try to put in a star shape or an explosive shape to make a pattern of jumping. Finish your pattern in a different shape from the one you started in. Practise until you are sure of the speed and form of your pattern.
2. Try again and this time, as you make your explosion or star, try to put in a sound to fit your movement. Work through your pattern again until you are sure you have the best possible sounds.
3. Put your body into a compact shape. When you hear the signal (gong) you are going to burst out of that shape. Decide which direction you are going to take, what shape you are going to be as you come out of your first shape and what position you are going to finish up in. Practise this several times before putting in the sound to fit your movement. Now try to make a different sound. What movement is going to fit this sound? Go back to your starting position and practise again, this time

knowing the sound first. Try once more, this time making a completely different shape, and taking a different path. Make more sounds if you wish and practise all your movements and sounds.

Play at 'Jack in the box'. Take up your position, wait for the signal to come out like Jack. Move as many parts of your body as you can when you are out. Make a sound as you come out. Do it in your own time without a signal.

4. Go back to your starting position. This time as you hear the 'unfolding' music (*steady, quiet rhythm on cymbal*), let your body come out and flow over like a volcano. Let as many parts of your body flow as you can. Can you try again with some other parts of your body leading the way out?

Join 3. and 4. together so that you have a flowing movement ending with an explosion. Hold your exploded position for a few seconds before letting it die away. Will it die away evenly? Change the order and start with an explosion ending with flowing movements.

5. Lie on the ground. When you hear the sharp tap on the cymbal, move your body or some part of it. Wait between taps: (they will be irregular and of different strengths).

Take up a different position to start—you may wrap up some part of your body, twist it, or start smaller, etc. Move again to the taps. Pick your best position and move without the taps, making your own noise as you do so.

This time move in a jerky way from your starting position until you hear the signal, then add an explosion.

Take up a starting position again. Begin with an explosion, as you have practised, and continue with irregular jerky movements until you die away.

6. Make a circular movement in the air. Show your body going in a circle in some way. Try with some other part of your body taking your weight. Move about the hall making round movements with your body. How are you going to move to join your circles together?

Work out a pattern of movement involving circles.

Work out a pattern now in a small space using two circular movements joined in any way you wish.

(*This should be extended to involve flowing movements and explosive movements joined to circular movements.*)

7. You have now tried a lot of movement shapes and joined them to others. Pick out three different ones. Practise them again to make sure you know what you are doing, then join them together in a pattern of your own.

(Music: Listen, Move and Dance No.4. H.M.V. CLP 3531.)

8. Now let's be fireworks. Think what sort of firework you are going to be —a banger, fountain, rip-rap, rocket, etc. Close your eyes and think carefully about your starting and finishing positions. When you are sure what you are going to be, start. Make noises to fit in.
   Try different sorts of fireworks.
   Work out a pattern of three different sorts of fireworks.

9. Work with a partner. One of you is going to light the firework and watch it, and the other is going to be the firework. Get a good starting position. Change over.

10. Work in a bigger group to give a firework display, with one person lighting the fireworks which go off one after the other, then all together. Don't forget that the person who lights them has a part to play. How might he react? What might happen to him when he hears a big bang or a jumping jack is near him?

Bonfires

1. *a.* Now think of the flames. Shut your eyes and see how the wood burns with the flames growing, shooting, spitting, flickering, reaching out, and dying away.

   b. Practise some body shapes like pieces of wood. Put your body in the shape of a piece of wood. Imagine the fire is starting to reach you, slowly at first with just a part of you on fire, then faster as the fire grows and you are all aflame. Try with some parts of your body starting to burn and other parts being big flames. After some time you are all burned up. What happens now? How will you finish up? Add some sounds if they will help.
   Try again with different starting positions. Remember all parts of your body will be burning. Be:
   > a small piece of wood that splutters and burns quickly
   > a large piece of wood that takes some time to be fully alight
   > a box or chair or something that collapses, either fully or in part, but still burns
   > a dry brittle piece that gives off a lot of sparks
   > a wet piece that just smoulders.

   Try to add some sounds to your movements.

2. *a.* Work as a class. Form yourselves into a bonfire shape with the small wood at the outside and larger wood towards the middle. Try to get some interesting individual shapes. The fire starts at the outside and after some time spreads to the middle, until the wood is all burning

fiercely and everyone is moving. Hold your positions until you think you catch fire. Parts of the fire will die away as it goes on. Make your sounds as you burn.

Try this in different positions.

b. Do this again but now some of you be fireworks outside the range of the fire. You needn't just be one firework or one kind of firework. Remember to keep your positions when you are not moving. Let the fire burn as it did before.

You now have a dance drama of a bonfire.

People and bonfires

As you know, a lot of other things happen at a bonfire, with people doing all sorts of things before, during, and after.

1. Build a bonfire. The wood is all around you. Sort it out, think about its shape, weight, and how you are going to move it into position. Make your pile ready for lighting.
2. Throw more wood on the fire and tend it as your parents do. Think how you would approach it to throw on more wood, or make it safe.
3. Put out a patch of fire that has spread.
4. Go up to the fire to put in some potatoes to roast. Wait for a while and then fish them out. You might have to search a little for them. Handle them with care.
5. Be given a hot, roasted potato and eat it.
6. Be a grown up at the fire:

> watching it
> lighting fireworks
> taking round food.

Practise again the part where some of you were the fire and others the fireworks. Add to it by having some being people as you have practised in **People and bonfires**. Decide what you are going to be and act through the bonfire scene.

Guy Fawkes

1. a. Take up a position for a Guy Fawkes on a bonfire. Move as you think he might as the fire comes to him and destroys part of his body.
   b. Work with a partner. One be a child and the other a Guy Fawkes. Let the child arrange the Guy in some position (Guy, think how your body is going to move), and try to attract attention and get money for him. Change over. Some of you go round and look at other children and their Guys. What are you going to do when you see them?
2. Be the real Guy Fawkes and creep into the cellars of the Houses of

Parliament to lay your barrels of gunpowder. Wait until the time comes for you to light them. Hear the guards coming along and hide.
3. Be a guard in the Houses of Parliament, hear a noise, and go to look. Find the barrels and decide what you are going to do. Show by your movements what you have decided.
4. Work in a group as guards moving through the cellars on inspection. Decide who is finally to make the discovery of the barrels and report it. All search again until you find Guy.
5. Have a few Guy Fawkes going through the scene as you did in 2. above. The rest be groups of guards who search the cellars and make the discovery. It doesn't matter how many there are. Talk it over first to decide how you are going to move, who is going to make the discovery, what you are going to do when you see him. Wait until all the Guys have settled down to hide before you begin to act through your part.

Written work

1. Write a story 'The Field that Comes to Life'. Think of what the field would be like in the November weather before the fire.
2. What was your bonfire like the morning after? How did you feel about it? Write a story or poem beginning 'The fire is out ...'
3. Tell the story of planting the gunpowder and being captured as if you were Guy Fawkes.
4. Tell the story from the point of view of someone else who was involved in it (e.g. another conspirator, who got away).
5. You will all have seen the N.S.P.C.A. notices about animals on Bonfire Night and how we have to look after them. Tell the story of a bonfire or a firework display as if you were an animal that had been there.
6. Make a list of the precautions you need to take to avoid trouble on Bonfire Night.
7. You have made firework shapes with your body. Pick a firework and try to make a poem in its shape.
8. Write a poem about fireworks. Think of the smells, sounds, and sights you have seen. Try to make it descriptive and powerful.
9. What was it like waiting for the bonfire to be lit? Write a poem or story called 'Before the Fire'.
10. Write about making a Guy, how you made it, and what you did with it. Make up a rhyme which would help you to get money for fireworks while showing your Guy.
11. Tell the story of the bonfire as if you were a Guy.

12. Write out and decorate any of the poems about bonfires and fireworks which have been read to you.
13. Can you write a poem consisting mostly of the sounds fireworks make? You can shape your poem to fit these sound words together and use other phrases to join them.

Animals

In every anthology for children there is a section on animals. The main difficulty of selection lies in the great quantity of poetry and prose. Much of this is sentimental writing by an adult for a completely unreal child and, as such, it should have no place in our reading. In this theme there are three stimuli we can give:

    a. Close observation of living creatures, carefully focused.

    b. Readings and dramatic work.

    c. Pictures and drawings.

Men and animals

Readings

The Kestrel	*Kes* (*A Kestrel for a Knave*).	Barry Hines
The Bet	*Call of the Wild* Ch.6	Jack London
Water Shrews	*King Solomon's Ring* Ch. 9	Konrad Z. Lorenz
The Bundle	*The Goshawk* Ch. 1	T. H. White
Training Animals	*Bandoola* Ch. 2	J. H. Williams
The Vet	Guy Boas	*The Pattern of Poetry*
Mrs Malone	Eleanor Farjeon	*All Day Long; A Puffin Quartet of Poets*
Our Local Zoo	Geoffrey Johnson	*Happenings* 1

Movement/drama

1. Read *Call of the Wild.*
   a. You are Thornton when Buck is about to pull the sledge. Think how you would move to encourage him and how you would show your feelings throughout the whole scene.

     b. All be Buck. Get into a good position for the pull. Think how you will use different parts of your body and how the speed of your movements will change.

     c. Work in pairs, one being Thornton, the other Buck. Think how they acted at the beginning and the end of the scene. Change over.

     d. Be onlookers watching the pull. You could be one who wants Buck to do it, or one who doesn't. You could be someone who is sure he won't, a person making or taking bets, an interested onlooker, a passer-by who gets caught up in the excitement. Make sure you decide who you are, then try again in a different role.

     e. Now work in larger groups with one Thornton, one Buck, and the rest as spectators (remember you all have a part to play).

2. Can you think of another scene where an animal does a feat of great strength for you? Talk it over first.

     a. You come across someone trapped by a falling tree or boulder. Hitch up your horse or dog and try to move the obstacle away. Show if you finally succeed.

     b. You are driving your dog team across the snow when your sledge slips into a crevasse. You manage to hold on and have to get the dogs to haul you up.

3. In *Bandoola* you heard how an elephant was broken in. How might other animals be trained?

     a. Train a dog to:

          respond to a signal

          guide a blind person across a road

          stay close to your heel as you walk

          run and then sit as you call him.

     b. Take a horse on a long rope. School him to:

          trot round in a circle

          reverse in tight circles

          walk along and rear up

          skip daintily over small obstacles

          anything else you have ever seen a trained horse do.

     Think of how you are going to control the horse. What are you going to use? What signals are you going to make?

4. Imagine someone brought a bundle to you as they did in *The Goshawk*. Show how you would approach it, unfasten it, and deal with the thing inside.

Written work

1. Tell the story of The Bet as though you were:
   a. Buck.
   b. An onlooker.
   c. Thornton.
2. Write an account of the progress you made training an animal. This could be in the form of a diary.
3. Do you think it is right for animals to be trained to do tricks for the circus, or even kept in zoos? (Read 'Our Local Zoo' by Geoffrey Johnson.)
4. How do you think the elephant was feeling as the man tried to get on his back? Be the elephant and tell the story. Why did you finally give in?
5. Tell the story of a man and an elephant doing something together. This might be to the benefit of the man, or of the elephant.

I Meeting animals

Readings

The Boy and the Bear	*When the Legends Die* Ch. 10, 18	Hal Borland
Helvi gets a Pet	*The Incredible Journey* Ch. 6	Sheila Burnford
Ben and the Puppies	*A Dog so Small* Ch.14	Philippa Pearce
Kim sees the horse	*Snow Cloud, Stallion* Ch. 12	Gerald Raftery
Young Puppies	*Warrior Scarlet* Ch. 3	Rosemary Sutcliff
The Runaway	Robert Frost	*All Day Long; The Golden Treasury of Poetry; Happenings* 1; *Enjoying Poetry* 1; *Birthright Poetry* 3; *The Faber Book of Children's Verse; The Oxford Book of Verse for Juniors* 3; *Selected Poems; The Key of the Kingdom* 2
Anne and the Field-mouse	Ian Serraillier	*Happily Ever After; Happenings* 1

To a Squirrel at Kyle-na-no   W. B. Yeats

*This Way Delight;
The Oxford Book of
Verse for Juniors 1;
The Key of the
Kingdom 2; The
Oxford Book of
Poetry for Children;
Wordscapes*

Movement/drama

1. Watch some puppies in a basket. Reach in and lift one out. Fondle the puppy. Try with a different animal. Stroke it. How does it feel?
2. Practise feeding very young animals. What are you going to use? How are you going to get them to take their food? Try different ways.
3. Watch an animal in the tree-tops. See it jump and swing.
4. How might you rescue an animal? Fetch a drowning dog from a stream. What are you going to do with it? Get a cat from up a tree or another animal from a trap. Think how you are going to move to give the animal confidence in you.
5. Try to coax a horse to come up to you. You might not succeed at first but keep trying.

Written work

1. Late at night you hear some scratching noises at the back door. Write an account of what you found and did.
2. Have you ever come across a stray animal, perhaps a puppy or kitten? Tell what it was like, how you felt, and what you did.
3. Write about a frightened animal you have met—perhaps a lost pet or some other animal you have seen. (Read again 'The Runaway' by Robert Frost.)
4. Tell the story about coming across an animal as Helvi or Kim did. Describe the animal as you would have seen him. How did you feel?
5. Have you ever been afraid of meeting an animal on your way somewhere, perhaps a dog in the neighbourbood you have to pass often or one you see on your way to school? What did the animal look like? Tell about it. In *Warrior Scarlet* Drem sees the new-born puppies and a great love springs up inside him for one of them. Have you ever seen any new-born animals? How did they seem to you and how did you feel? Did 'strange things happen inside' you as they did to him?

7. Try to think of the first time you touched a particular animal and felt some part of it (perhaps a bird's claw, a hamster's feet on your hand, a donkey's or horse's nose taking some food from you). How did it feel at first and how did your feelings develop?
8. Tell the story of how you met and made friends with a strange animal (Read *A Stranger at Green Knowe* by L. M. Boston).
9. Does any animal ever come to you—a dog on your bed, a cat on your lap, a budgie on your shoulder? Tell about it.
10. On T.V. films and series you see and hear of a great many children and grown-ups who have a much greater chance of meeting animals than you do. Would you like to be one of them? Which one would you be and what would you do?

II Watching animals

Readings

Wild Cats	*Seal Morning* Ch. 10	Rowena Farre
The Fish	*Ring of Bright Water* Ch. 16	Gavin Maxwell
Elver's Migration	*Ring of Bright Water* Ch. 16	Gavin Maxwell
To Sparrows Fighting	W. H. Davies	*Twentieth Century Poetry*
Fox	Clifford Dyment	*The Harrap Book of Modern Verse*
Trout	Seamus Heaney	*The Death of a Naturalist; Thoughtshapes*
The Fox	Phoebe Hesketh	*The Harrap Book of Modern Verse; Enjoying Poetry* 6
Turf Carrier on Aranmore	J. Hewitt	*Voices* 1
Little Fish	D. H. Lawrence	*Voices* 1
Frogs	Norman MacCaig	*Voices* 3
Fish in the Pacific	Ian Serraillier	*The Ballad of Kon-Tiki, and other verses*
Fish	W. W. E. Ross	*Wordscapes*
January	R. S. Thomas	*Penguin New Poetry*
The World below the Brine	Walt Whitman	*Junior Voices* 4

Movement/drama

1. Take up your position to watch:
   a. Fish in a stream or pond. Reach in very gently with your hand and try to get one. Watch again as the water settles.
   b. Some animals playing. Try to take a photograph or moving film of the scene.
   c. Animals in a fight.
   d. Animals about to attack you. Read about the children in *Children on the Oregon Trail* by A. Rutgers Van der Loeff and act this scene through.
2. You are watching a herd of wild horses, waiting for the best moment to try to lassoo one of them. Watch for the opportunity to throw your lassoo. Think what is going to happen and how you are going to approach the horse.
3. Gavin Maxwell tells of watching a large number of elvers moving. Watch another large collection of animals. React to:

   > wasps at a picnic
   > elephants charging
   > fish swimming into a net
   > horses stampeding.

4. You see a bird trying to fly but it is injured and cannot get off the ground. Watch it carefully to try to decide what is wrong, and when you think the time is right, approach it and show what you do to calm it; put it right, and perhaps set it free. Now try the same thing with another animal.
5. Move as you would:

   > in fish-filled water
   > in pools, paddling and watching for jelly-fish
   > through a swarm of bees
   > in a cave where bats have rested
   > in shallow water where crocodiles live
   > in snake-infested grass
   > in a field where cows and bulls are grazing
   > in a compound of stray dogs, while looking for your own dog
   > in a lane, leading a donkey which is doing a job (read 'Turf Carrier on Aranmore' by J. Hewitt).

Written work

1. Watch any animal carefully and write a poem about how it moves. This could be:

> fish in a bowl
> a bird in a cage
> a mouse
> a rat
> a donkey pulling a cart
> a donkey taking children for a ride
> an animal at the zoo
> flies and moths round a light
> birds in flight.

2. Write about an animal fight you have seen. (Read 'To Sparrows Fighting' by W. H. Davies.)
3. Tell the story of the wild cats (*Seal Morning*) or the sea full of fish (*Ring of Bright Water*) as if you had been there.
4. Which animal do you like watching most? Tell about it, and why you like watching it. What is special about this animal?
5. In 'January', R.S. Thomas tells of when he watched a wounded fox moving over the snow. Have you ever seen an injured animal? Write about what it looked like and how you felt.
6. Watch an animal:

> eating its food
> feeding or caring for its young
> washing itself
> playing.

Write about what you saw. Think about the movements, noise, speed. Pick out the most striking aspect and concentrate on that.

III Cats and dogs

These are by far the most popular domestic animals and one hopes that, if children are given plenty of readings, movement, and chances of observation, the resultant writing will be of a higher standard than that often found under the title 'My Pet'.

Readings

The Dogs	*The Incredible Journey* Sheila Burnford Ch. 1
The Dog Boy	*The Sword in the Stone* T. H. White Ch. 5

The Cat	Richard Church	*Birthright Poetry 2;* *All Day Long; Mood* *and Rhythm 3*
Cat in the Long Grass	Alan Dixon	*A Flock of Words*
Man and Beast	C. Dyment	*As Large As Alone*
The Naming of Cats	T. S. Eliot	*The Albemarle Book* *of Modern Verse 1*
Growltiger's Last Stand	T. S. Eliot	*Happenings 1; The* *Faber Book of* *Children's Verse*
McCavity the Mystery Cat	T. S. Eliot	*Old Possum's Book* *of Practical Cats*
Cat!	Eleanor Farjeon	*Happenings 1;* *Enjoying Poetry 6;* *Rhyme and Rhythm* (red); *Mood and* *Rhythm 2; Poetry and* *Life 3; The Oxford* *Book of Poetry for* *Children; A Puffin* *Quartet of Poets;* *Silver-Sand and Snow*
A Dog in the Quarry	Miroslav Holub	*Selected Poems;* *Junior Voices 4*
Lament of a Poor Blind	Thomas Hood	*The Penguin Book of* *Animal Verse*
Esther's Tomcat	Ted Hughes	*The Penguin Book of* *Animal Verse;* *Penguin New Poetry*
The Tom-Cat	Don Marquis	*Pegasus 1; Poetry and* *Life 4; Junior Voices* 4.
Diamond Cut Diamond	Ewart Milne	*The Faber Book of* *Children's Verse;* *Harrap's Junior Book* *of Modern Verse*
Milk for the Cat	Harold Monro	*The Book of a* *Thousand Poems;* *Round the Day; My* *Kind of Verse; This* *Way Delight; The* *Golden Treasury of* *Poetry*
Catalogue	Rosalie Moore	*The Golden Treasury* *of Poetry*

Lone Dog	Irene R. McLeod	*All Day Long; Happenings* 1; *Mood and Rhythm* 1
Child on Top of a Greenhouse	T. Roethke	*The Oxford Book of Verse for Juniors* 4; *Junior Voices* 3
My Cat Jeoffry	Christopher Smart	*The Faber Book of Children's Verse; An Anthology of Free Verse; Mystery, Magic and Adventure; The Oxford Book of Poetry for Children; The Golden Treasury of Poetry*
Dog	William Jay Smith	*The Golden Journey*
Windy Boy in a Windswept Tree	G. Summerfield	*The Oxford Book of Verse for Juniors* 4
The Rescue	Hal Summers	*Dawn and Dusk*
Cats	A. S. J. Tessimond	*All Day Long; The Albemarle Book of Modern Verse* 1; *Pegasus* 4
A Cat	Edward Thomas	*Enjoying Poetry* 6

Movement/drama

1. Play with your cat or dog.
2. Practise grooming your cat or dog. Think of all the things you will have to do to make your pet clean and shining.
3. Get a dog or cat ready for a pet show. When you are ready:
   a. Set your cat up for the judge to see.
   b. Parade your dog in front of the judges:
      make it walk
      make it trot
      order your dog away and bring it back to heel.
   c. Some of you be judges while the others parade or stand with their dogs for you to look at them. Examine the dogs carefully and be sure of what you are looking for. You might have to tell the owner to do certain things for you while you judge.
4. A cat is stranded up a high tree. How could you rescue it? The cat is frightened and is hard to get. Act through the little scene of hearing miaowing, finding where the cat is, going to rescue it, setting it free. (Read 'Windy Boy in a Windswept Tree' by Geoffrey Summerfield,

'Child on Top of a Greenhouse' by Theodore Roethke, and 'The Rescue' by Hal Summers.)

5. You are giving a dog a bath. Act through the scene, thinking of all the difficulties you will probably have.

6. Practise these 'body shapes'. That is, put your body into the shape you think a cat would when:

> it is very angry
> it is stalking something
> it is about to catch a mouse
> it is lying in front of the fire
> it is curled up in a chair
> it is stretching itself after waking
> it is watching a bowl of goldfish.

Practise each one several times to get your best shape.

7. Be a cat:

> washing itself
> trying to get through a locked door
> slinking through a narrow gap
> rubbing itself against someone's legs
> sharpening its claws
> jumping a wide gap
> picking its way across a muddy patch
> fighting another cat (don't forget the noises).

8. Show what happens when you meet a dog.

Written work

1. Watch a cat very closely as he comes to some milk; on the prowl for birds.
   Was there any difference in the way it moved on these two occasions? Was it patient, careful, cunning? Write a poem to bring out the quality of the movement.

2. Tell the story of 'The Pet Show', 'The Rescue' or 'The Bath' (**Movement/ drama**, 3., 4., and 5., see p.116)

3. Read again 'Catalogue' by Rosalie Moore. Write a 'dogalogue'.

4. Which is the most unusual cat or dog you have ever seen? Describe it.

5. How did you get your pet? Tell the story of what happened.

6. Listen again to 'Lament of a Poor Blind' by Thomas Hood. Can you make up a similar piece about cats?

7. Write a story about how a cat and a dog became friends.

8. Read again any of the poems in T. S. Eliot's *Old Possum's Book of Practical Cats.* Can you do the same for dogs by writing up some imaginary unusual dogs and their doings?
9. 'A dog is a man's best friend.' Do you think this is true? What advantage has a cat over a dog or a dog over a cat as a pet?

IV Small animals

Readings

There be four things that are little	*The Holy Bible* (Proverbs, Ch.30, v.24)	
The Ants	John Clare	*The Wood is Sweet*
Earth-worm	Leonard Clark	*Daybreak*
Little Things	James Stephens	*The Golden Journey*
The Prayer of the Lizard	Carmen Bernos de Gasztold	*The World Around*
Spider Webs	Ray Fabrizio	*My Kind of Verse*
Considering the Snail	Thom Gunn	*Common Ground; A Flock of Words*
Spider's Little City	R. Heron	*American Poetry, An Introductory Anthology*
The Snail	James Reeves	*A Puffin Quartet of Poets; Blackwell's Junior Poetry Book* 4; *The Oxford Book of Poetry for Children; The Key of the Kingdom* 1
Rendez-vous with a Beetle	E. V. Rieu	*A Puffin Quartet of Poets; Poetry and Life* 3
Worms and the Wind	Carl Sandburg	*The Albemarle Book of Modern Verse* 1
The Garden Snail	R. Wallace	*Wordscapes; Happenings* 1
A Noiseless Patient Spider	Walt Whitman	*Birds, Beasts, and Fishes*
Hibernating Snails	Andrew Young	*Collected Poems*

Movement/drama

1. Explore as many ways as possible of making a web. Think carefully of your pattern in the air and on the floor. Let different parts of your body lead the movements (*Music*: The Rite of Spring *by Stravinsky*). Think what the spider might be doing:

> hanging from a thread
> climbing up a thread
> running swiftly to attack
> weaving round his captive.

After you have practised different ways, pick out your best dance, and practise that. Think of the different speeds of movement. When you have finished your web, think how you are going to move across the filaments. How are you going to approach and inspect your prey before making the final attack?

2. Be an insect caught in a web. How are you going to move? What is going to happen as different parts of your body become entwined in the web? How are you going to finish up? Practise as many positions of being caught at the end as you can.

3. Join 1. and 2. together for a dance drama on an insect being caught in a spider's web.

4. Make up as many different body shapes as you can for each of these creatures: spiders, worms, beetles, snails.

5. When you have got your best position, move as if you were the creature. Let different parts of your body lead the way.

Written work

Before beginning the written work, the teacher should draw attention to particular facets of these creatures: the industry and organization of the ants; the revulsion people sometimes feel for spiders, worms, and beetles; the peculiar movements of snails and tortoises, and so on.

1. In 'The Prayer of a Lizard' the animal is asking for the things which suit him best. Write a similar piece for any of the others. What would be their idea of Paradise?

2. Write in prose or poetry about 'little things' and their world.

3. Write a poem about any small creature. Try to give your poem a shape like the creature.

4. '... and frightened Miss Muffet away'. Why should it be a spider? Do they frighten you? Why do they frighten some people do you think? What sort of person do you imagine Miss Muffet was?

5. Write a story as if you were the spider. Tell how you frightened Miss Muffet away.

6. Pick out any striking phrase from the poems you have read. For example:

> ... He
> moves on his
>   single
> Elastic Foot ...

or

> ... climbing
>   all afternoon
> with his brown shell
>   up the wobbly tall
>   grass.
>   (both from 'The Garden Snail', by R. Wallace)

Try to think of other phrases to describe these creatures.

V Protection and care

Readings

The Rescue	*The Singing Forest* Ch. 2	H. M. Batten
Auguries of Innocence	William Blake	*The Faber Book of Children's Verse; Birds, Beasts and Fishes; My Kind of Verse; The Penguin Book of Animal Verse*
Little Things	James Stephens	*The Golden Journey*
The Bells of Heaven	Ralph Hodgson	*The Golden Journey; Rhyme and Rhythm* (yellow); *Mood and Rhythm* 1; *The Book of a Thousand Poems*
Hurt no Living Thing	Christina Rossetti	*The Merry-Go-Round; Poetry and Life* 1; *Rhyme and Rhythm* (blue)
Anne and the Field-mouse	Ian Serraillier	*Happenings* 1; *Happily Ever After*
Death of a Bird	Jon Silkin	*Thoughtshapes; As Large as Alone*

| Caring for Animals | Jon Silkin | *Harrap's Junior Book of Modern Verse* |
| The Beasts | Walt Whitman | *Birds, Beasts and Fishes; My Kind of Verse; Mood and Rhythm 4; Enjoying Poetry 6* |

VI Familiar animals

Readings

The Lamb	William Blake	*The Golden Treasury of Poetry; The Book of a Thousand Poems; Poetry Panorama 2; The Oxford Book of Verse for Juniors 1; The Faber Book of Children's Verse*
The Donkey	G. K. Chesterton	*Mood and Rhythm 4; Rhyme and Rhythm (yellow); Enjoying Poetry 6*
Nicholas Nye	Walter de la Mare	*Pegasus 1; The Merry-Go-Round; The Book of a Thousand Poems; Enjoying Poetry 6; The Oxford Book of Poetry for Children*
The Colt	Raymond Knister	*The Oxford Book of Verse for Juniors 4*
At Grass	Philip Larkin	*Dawn and Dusk; The Pattern of Poetry*
Horses	Edwin Muir	*The Faber Book of Children's Verse; All Day Long*
Cows	James Reeves	*A Puffin Quartet of Poets*
The Squirrel	Ian Serraillier	*The Oxford Book of Verse for Juniors 4; A Puffin Quartet of Poets; All Day Long*
Hedgehog	Anthony Thwaite	*Happenings 1*
The Stallion	Walt Whitman	*The Oxford Book of Verse for Juniors 4*
Man and Cows	Andrew Young	*Collected Poems*

VII Fantastic and humorous

Readings

		How the Whale Became Ted Hughes
The Common Cormorant	Anon.	*The Faber Book of Children's Verse*
The Zobo Bird	Frank A. Collymore	*The Golden Journey*
The Hippocrump	James Reeves	*Happenings* 1
The Unicorn	E. V. Rieu	*A Puffin Quartet of Poets*
Meditation of a Tortoise	E. V. Rieu	*A Puffin Quartet of Poets*

VIII Snakes and reptiles

Readings

The Giant Snake	*Zoo Quest for a Dragon* Ch. 3	David Attenborough
Heracles and The Snakes	*The Golden Shadow* Ch. 3	Edward Blishen and Leon Garfield
Snakes	*Creatures Moving* (ed. G. Summerfield)	Penguin English Project, Stage One
Snake Phobia	*Creatures Moving*	Penguin English Project, Stage One
A Narrow Fellow in the Grass	Emily Dickinson	*All Day Long; The Key of the Kingdom* 4; *A Flock of Words*
To the Snake	Denise Levertov	*Voices* 2
The Viper	Ruth Pitter	*Dawn and Dusk; All Day Long; Birthright Poetry* 4
In the Snake Park	William Plomer	*Every Man Will Shout*
Snakes	A. K. Ramanujan	*Thoughtshapes*
Snake	Theodore Roethke	*Wordscapes*
Song	William Shakespeare	*Poetry and Life* 2; *This Way Delight; The Oxford Book of Verse for Juniors* 2; *My Kind of Verse*
The Snake	Valerie (aged 8)	*Junior Voices* 1

Circuses and Fairs

It would be hard to find a theme with greater possibilities for art and craft, or one with such a natural appeal for movement/drama as this. I have yet to meet a child who was not excited at the thought of a circus or fair. There are great possibilities too for free movement (defined as a child's undirected response to a stimulus, in this case probably music) and so for improvised play making and mime.

For craft the possibilities are almost limitless. Children could work on a circus or fair project with painting, models, masks, noses for clowns, plates, skittles, hoops for jugglers, head-dresses, hats, frills, animal costumes, posters for advertising, tickets, and invitations to other classes to attend the circus, and so on.

Those teachers who feel that animal acts in circuses should not be encouraged could leave out the section on animal trainers, or utilize it in a way that leads children to discuss the ethics of animal training—what is legitimate and what is to be resisted. Some children might like to do research about circuses: how the animals are caged, fed, cared for, trained, transported, stabled; what happens to the circus in winter; its history; its movements and routes; the lives of the circus performers, and so on. Similarly, different aspects of fairs can be investigated, along with medieval fairs, quack doctors, country fairs, etc.

Readings

Dido at the Fair	*Black Hearts in Battersea* Ch. 9	Joan Aiken
The Fairground	*Thimble Summer* Ch. 8	Elizabeth Enright
The Bull Dances of Knossos	*The 22 Letters* Ch. 7	Clive King
The Strong Man	*The Little Tumbler* Ch. 3	Eleanor Frances Lattimore
Wang the Conjuror	*The Little Tumbler* Ch. 3	Eleanor Frances Lattimore

Movement/drama and mime

General

1. Move as your would:
    a. Through a crowd of people at a fairground. Show what you are watching from time to time.
    b. While collecting the fares on a moving roundabout.
    c. Trying to hustle people into having a go on your stall.
    d. Leading some circus animals. Try with different ones.
    e. Selling some ice-cream or hot dogs from a tray you are carrying.
    f. Blowing up balloons and twisting them into shapes to sell.
    g. Directing the heavy circus traffic into the field.
    h. Bedding down the animals, grooming, and feeding them.
    i. Working in groups to erect the heavy tents.
    j. Driving in the stakes and pegs.
    k. Reparing and repainting some of the equipment.
    l. Erecting the roundabout.
    m. Working the swing boats as an attendant, or riding them.
2. Let's mime some fairground pleasures. Here are a few suggestions:
    a. Throw the rings at a hoopla stall.
    b. Shoot at balls, clay-pipes, or targets with a rifle.
    c. Throw darts at playing cards.
    d. Throw balls into bowls.
    e. Have a go on the coconut shy.
    f. Drive a dodgem car.
    g. Try your strength. Can you ring the bell with the mallet?

Class drama

The practices which follow are designed to give children movement experience on this theme. The order does not matter nor does the sequence of building them up into a class performance. There is no reason whatever why, at different times during the progress of the experience, such parts as have been practised separately should not be put together into an arbitrary sequence. That is to say, children may choose their parts from the practices they have had at any stage—some be this and some that, and respond when the signals are given. (The signals may only be the teacher calling out 'Now, we will have the . . . , now the . . . ') The music keys are very important but are not as difficult as might be imagined by the non-technical or non-musical. If a pianist is available to play the keying music when calls are made, so much the better; if recordings can be made, better still. If not, simple percussion patterns by the teacher will fill the bill very well. Most of the music demands a climax which is very easy with a cymbal or drum, prefaced by some rolling. If these keys are used early, say after the first two practices, then the children will come to know what is expected and respond when the signals are given. Children can, in fact, easily make their own music with chime bars and percussion, with some providing the music and others doing the movement. They can then work in groups on the movement practices. The important thing is that the patterns should be constant and well-known. The use of a tape recorder would be ideal.

General

First of all practise coming into the circus ring to the cheers and applause of the audience. Receive and acknowledge their cheers. Come in in different ways: as though you were with a partner; leading something; pushing or carrying something; with some special equipment, and so on. Remember it is a big ring and the audience is all around you.

Be the ring master and walk in as he would. Make your gestures big and expressive.

Now each of the following acts has three parts. Each one is different and you will have to remember to move as fits your character in each of these parts. They are: the entry; the act; and the exit.

The strong man

1. Come into the ring as the strong man would and show your magnificent physique. Take up different positions to show the strength in various parts of your body. Hold your poses.

    Before you go into your act, remember to work slowly up to the climax. (*Music with a crescendo, perhaps a rolling cymbal beat.*)

    Hold your position, and come out of it as the strong man would. Practise:

    > lifting weights
    > lifting something with various parts of your body (teeth, legs, arms, etc.)
    > lifting a person on each arm
    > bending an iron bar over various parts of your body
    > supporting weights on your back, tummy, legs in the air, etc.
    > ripping something
    > pulling something (try different positions all the time).

    Pick out your three best stunts and work them into an act. Remember to pause and take the applause between each one. Make your exit and wait for the others to finish.

3. Some of you be strong men and the others photographers.

Make a viewer with your hands and go round taking photographs of the strong men doing their acts. Try from different positions and ask them to hold it if you want them to. Change over.
4. Work in a group. One of you is to be the strong man and the others to be a small section of the audience. Get close together and see if you can respond to the strong man as he goes through his act.

The jugglers
(Music: your own, or 'The Jugglers' from Stravinsky's Petrushka.)
1. Practise juggling with imaginary objects.
2. Balance a ball on the back of your neck, juggle with three more balls, then with a flick bring the ball on your neck into the juggling.
3. Can you work out a routine using other parts of your body as well as your hands? Try to alter the speed of your work so that at times you are still.
4. Put the objects you are juggling with in other places as well as in the air; e.g. you might roll some along your arm or down your back, or you might include a sequence of bouncing.
5. Do something such as turning, rolling, lying down, as you juggle.
6. Can you make it into a rather comic act? You might do something else while juggling:

> read a book and juggle with one hand
> be very tired or bored and lean against something
> take a drink and juggle with one hand
> take off your coat while juggling.

Can you think of other things to do while juggling? Show them.
7. Let something go wrong while you are doing your act. Show what happens.
8. Juggle in slow motion.
9. As before, pick out your three best juggling tricks and work them into an act. Start from where you come in and end by taking the cheers and going off.
10. Be jugglers, photographers, and audience as before.
11. Work with a partner, juggling in twos. Try to make your act interesting by doing different things. Talk it over first. If you are using anything dangerous or unusual (e.g. flaming torches), don't forget to show this fully to the audience.
12. Can you work out a juggling act, or an act where things are kept in the air, which takes you to different parts of the ring as you go through your act?

Knife throwers

(Music: rolls and crashes.)

1. Come in and show your knives to the audience.
2. With plenty of gestures and taking your time, throw your knives at the target. Show when you have completed what you set out to do.
3. Work out an act with a partner. One of you is to be the assistant who blindfolds the thrower, leads him to his place, and hands him another knife each time he has thrown one. Do it slowly with much gesturing and take up a position while he goes through his act. Both show when the act is over. If you talk it over first you might be able to decide on a target for the thrower.
4. Let the partner take up a position. Work through a sequence where the knife thrower blindfolds the partner and throws the knives around him. You both have a part to play.
5. Let the partner stand with a cigarette in his mouth (make a show of putting it in and lighting it), and the thrower cut off the end with a knife.

Tightrope walkers

(Waltz music)

1. Walk along a high wire. Are you holding anything? Move forward, sideways, backwards. Make the wire bounce up and down while you keep your balance. Alter the speed of your moving so that you run or hop along the wire. Alter your position so that you are not always moving along standing up.
2. Add a pretended stumble or misfooting to your movements. Struggle to regain your balance.
3. Do something with another part of your body as you move along the wire. Try kneeling down, for example.
4. How about ballet dancing or aerobatics on the high wire?
5. Watch each other's work so far.
6. Listen to the music and, using any of the things you have done so far, try to work out a dance on the wire. Practise this until you are sure of your sequence.
7. You are going to finish your act with one stupendous feat. Think what it is going to be—a leap and twist, the splits, a cartwheel along the wire, as examples. Practise it by yourself. Begin slowly so that the audience feel the difficulty of what you are attempting.
8. The music will stop, there will be a roll, and you will do your last trick, ending as the cymbal crashes. Come down from the wire (you might

think of an individual ending to this), receive your applause, and leave
the ring.
9. Put these together now as a complete act, starting from your entrance
and getting on the wire. Remember your finish.

Animal trainers

1. Go into the lions' cage and put them through their tricks. Think how
you are going to control them and be very sure what they are going to
do. One of the lions becomes very threatening to you and seems to be
upsetting the others. What are you going to do?
2. Try with elephants. How will this be different from dealing with the
lions? Lie down and get an elephant to step over you; make the elephants
stand on small boxes and sit down when you command them; make them
get in a line and rise on two legs. Can they make a pyramid? What else
could you do with them?
3. Have the liberty horses in the ring and go through an act with them.
4. There are plenty of other animals used in circuses—dogs, chimps,
monkeys, snakes, bears, seals, etc. Be the trainer of any group of
animals and put them through an act. Think of the things they could
do and the apparatus they might use. Don't forget the beginning, climax,
and end of your act. It might help if you write down the things you are
going to get them to do and plan it out.

Clowns

This area has great possibilities for exercises in improvisation and mime.
Older children could well look into the traditions and history of circus
clowning, and the lives of famous clowns. They could be asked for more
specific comic mimes—sometimes concentrating on detail, sometimes on
imagination, sometimes on dramatic effects. They could, for example, find
a comic ending to destroy belief in the mime created (see Chapter 17,
Sampson's Circus). Below is a list of activities from which choice can be
made.

1. Walk like a clown coming into the ring. Try different ways of walking
in an exaggerated way. Pick your best way.
2. Put in a stumble, attempt to right it, and fall.
3. When you fall this time, let something happen. You might fall backwards
into water, or forwards, with your face ending in something.
4. Come in carrying something. Stumble and try to balance, and stop it
falling over you. Try to bring the audience into it by threatening to let
it fall over some of them. Fail in your attempt to save yourself.
5. Work with a partner, one as a clown playing an instrument or doing a
trick and the other coming in with a load. Where is it going to fall this
time?

6. Be two clowns trying to start a motor car. Talk it over first, and work out a sequence in which you will finish with nothing but a pile of metal and a terrible mess.
7. Can you work out a clown sequence where a group of clowns are: baking; decorating a room; taking a photograph; playing in a band; in any other situation you can think of.
8. Be a clown and try to work out a sequence with a musical instrument where things happen.
9. Dance like a clown (*Music: The Circus Clown's Dance' from* Petrushka *by Stravinsky*). Can you add some comic movements, like throwing a bucket of water, or getting a pie in your face to your dance?

The circus performance
Before beginning, time should be spent in the classroom, discussing the order of items; how they are going to be introduced; what help is needed with the music and what form the presentation will be in (i.e. what entrances and exits are required); who is to do what. There is no reason at all why children should not do more than one thing, if they list what is decided, so that everyone knows what is going to happen. There should be a quick run-through first, with everyone playing each part, as it is called out or the cues given.

1. Decide what parts you are going to play.
2. Begin with the grand parade, where you walk round, showing yourselves to the audience. (*Music:* Bolero *by Ravel*)
3. Go through the circus performance.

Written work

1. Listen to 'Elephants in a circus'. What do the animals in the circus look like to you?
2. Would you like to be the man who works a roundabout? What do you think about them and the world they live in?
3. Make a list of all the things clowns do. Pick out one of the things and make up a verse about that.
4. Describe the lights at the fair in a poem.
5. Tell about one of the things you saw at Stourbridge Fair (*Brother Dusty-Feet*) as though you were there.
6. Do you think Argos would have a different opinion of Stourbridge Fair? Tell his story of the fair.
7. Can you write a poem about jugglers? You might be able to arrange the words of your poem in a way that will help the impression.

8. What does it feel like when the circus or fair has left? Write a piece beginning, 'The circus has gone ... '
9. Have you ever been on a ferris wheel at a fair? What does the fairground look like when you are high up?
10. Would you like to work at a fair or with a circus? Tell what you would like to do and what you would like about it most of all.
11. Describe any character from a circus: Samson the strong man; Marvo the Magician; Madame Hie the Fortune Teller, or any other you can think of.
12. Write a poem about the Hall of Mirrors or the Ghost Train.
13. In 'Fairgrounds', Dylan Thomas says that fairs are no good in the daytime. Describe the change that comes over them at night.
14. Tell the story of when you won a prize at a fair. If you had a choice, was it easy to decide what to pick?
15. Can you arrange a poem in the shape of a helter skelter or slide, making the poem tell what it is like on one?
16. Have you ever given a performance in your shed or backyard with a group of other children? Tell about it.

War

Some teachers may feel that this is not a suitable topic for children. I can see no reason for avoiding it if the points made previously about the function of the teacher are accepted. Children are exposed to constant scenes of war, fighting, and suffering on television news and films. Poetry and prose provide a different approach to the war theme which will help them to 'place', or further assess, this material and to retain sensitivity and emotional responsiveness. When writing about the wider aspects of war, authors are dealing with personal emotions at a deep and basic level, and though in many of the extracts courage and daring are celebrated, invariably the tragedy of war is also brought home. Children responding to these extracts realize that human beings are involved and can identify closely. This is a situation we must exploit to minimize the effects of many comics and pulp productions. A teacher, through judicious selection, can give this theme the emphasis most suited to the level of maturity of the class, and can emphasize the excitement and bravery, the waste and destruction, or the high level of personal relationships, as seems most appropriate.

Readings

Night Bombing Flight	*The Perilous Descent: Into a Strange Lost World* Ch. 1	Bruce Carter
The Planes	*The House of Sixty Fathers* Ch. 1	Meindert De Jong
The Ambush	*Drummer Boy* Ch. 1	Leon Garfield
The Chase in the Wood	*Drummer Boy* Ch. 14	Leon Garfield
The Attack	*King Solomon's Mines* Ch. 13	Sir.H. Rider Haggard
The Last Stand of the Greys	*King Solomon's Mines* Ch. 14	Sir H. Rider Haggard
The Parachute Drop	*There's No Escape* Ch. 3	Ian Serraillier

The Battle of Hattin	*Knight Crusader* Ch. 8	Ronald Welch
Chant before Battle	Anon.	*Voices* 1
Roman Wall Blues	W. H. Auden	*Dawn and Dusk; My Kind of Verse; Harrap's Junior Book of Modern Verse; Junior Voices* 4
The Destruction of Sennacherib	Lord Byron	*The Faber Book of Children's Verse; The Pilgrim Book of Verse* 2; *Blackwell's Junior Poetry Book* 4; *Mood and Rhythm* 4
Hohenlinden	Thomas Campbell	*The Pilgrim Book of Verse* 1
The Unconcerned	Thomas Flatman	*The Faber Book of Children's Verse*
War Song of the Saracens	James Elroy Flecker	*Other Men's Flowers*
The Fall of Troy	Miroslav Holub	*Selected Poems*
Advice to a Knight	T. H. Jones	*A Flock of Words*
	John Masefield	*A Tale of Troy;* (extract, 'The Surprise', in *The Albemarle Book of Modern Verse* 1)
Exposure	Wilfred Owen	*Every Man Will Shout*
The War Song of Dinas Vawr	Thomas Love Peacock	*Blackwell's Junior Poetry Book* 4; *The Faber Book of Children's Verse; Poetry Panorama* 4; *Exploring Poetry* 4
The Dug-Out	Siegfried Sassoon	*Come Hither; A Flock of Words*
Pibroch of Donhuil Dhu	Sir Walter Scott	*The Faber Book of Children's Verse; The Pilgrim Book of Verse* 1; *Pegasus* 2; *Junior Voices* 3
The Massacre of Glencoe	Sir Walter Scott	*The Pilgrim Book of Verse* 2
St. Crispin's Day	William Shakespeare	*Henry V* . Act IV, Sc.3

Parachute	Stanley Snaith	*The Harrap Book of Modern Verse*
The Burial of Sir John Moore at Corunna	Charles Wolfe	*The Pilgrim Book of Verse* 1; *Common Ground; Mood and Rhythm* 3
An Irish Airman Foresees His Death	W. B. Yeats	*The Faber Book of Children's Verse; The Golden Journey; Other Men's Flowers*

Movement/drama

The story of the horse (*A Tale of Troy*)

1. *a.* Be the soldiers working:
      making the horse
      pushing it into position on the beach
      mending the palisades
      digging the ditches
      on night patrol
      caring for the sick
      preparing to camp for the night.
   b. Develop this further into a soldier's life in more modern times:
      being on guard
      throwing grenades
      lining up and searching prisoners
      on patrol through a riot area
      working as a team firing a large gun
      creeping up to a position and then attacking it.
2. Suspect a man of being a traitor and watch him without arousing his suspicions. Follow him and show how you would react. Try to imagine him in as many situations as you can; he may get up when everyone else is asleep; he may try to sneak off. You may have to undo some of his work.

Class drama

The city captured (*A Tale of Troy*)

The drama will evolve rather than be set. Children should be given choice of the parts they are to play, after practice and experience in them all, and should be encouraged to widen their parts as much as possible. The extract

must be read several times so that the children are familiar with the story.
I would suggest practice and progression on these lines:

1. 'Set forth towards Troy. Move along as you think the soldiers would.
   Remember the darkness, the need for silence, the wind 'beating the
   withered grass and shrivelled leaves'. Do you travel over different sorts
   of ground? Are you always at the same speed? How do you know where
   you are going?
2. 'Creep along like ghosts'. Are you always upright when you travel? Rest
   as you would in the bitter cold. Imagine your garments and how you
   might try to keep warm by moving parts of your body. Always remember the city in the distance. Huddle together in small groups in the bitter
   cold weather.
3. Work in groups now to practise all this sequence as far as the resting
   place. Move together in the same direction and settle down for the wait
   as a group. Talk it over first to decide how you are going to move, in
   what formation you will be.
4. All act the part of the messenger going to Diomed.
5. Be the person within the gate (Odysseus) lifting down the bar of the
   gate and opening it.
6. Work in groups. One will be inside and the others waiting outside. One
   be Diomed. Take the poem from 'Then suddenly there came a little noise'
   to 'It was Odysseus, from the Horse'. How do the ones outside respond
   to the gate beginning to open? Move up to get the gate fully opened and
   go in. Change places to practise this scene again.
7. Be the people inside the town, some dead 'newly murdered there', some
   'drowsy horse-boys mumbling in their sleep', some guards who see the
   Greeks and decide they are Lycians. Practise this several times in different positions and being different people each time.
8. Work in groups to combine 6. and 7. with the Trojans inside the city.
   Diomed and his followers enter and the action continues. Respond to
   each other as you think they would do.
9. Work with a partner, one to be the sentry who challenged too late and
   the other Diomed.
10. Get into groups and be guards sleeping in Apollo's temple. Think how
    you might move when the Greeks burst in. How would you waken?
    What might you try to do? Make the groups bigger and some be the
    Greeks surprising the guards, 'herd them like sheep', and bind them up.
11. Be young Delphobus 'fighting for his life with twelve'. Think how you
    will move during the fight and at the end of it.

(After individual and group practises on these lines the teacher could begin to draw the parts together for a class drama. Several actions will be going on at the same time and plenty of discussion with the children will be needed.)

Movement/drama

Parachute drop

1. Move as you think a man would with all his parachute equipment on.
2. Sit in the aeroplane and practise checking your kit through. Go over the things in your mind which you have to memorize.
3. Be the despatcher in the aeroplane, think of the checking you have to do. Get the jumpers into line and on the rope; open the hatch or door; watch for the signal light; and order your men to jump.
4. Practise jumping and landing from different things:
    a. Jumping from a moving bus.
    b. Jumping on to a moving bus.
    c. Jumping off a wall or tree (think how you would land).
    d. Get into a standing position. Jump off something, and roll.
    e. Jump on and off a moving staircase.
    f. Get into the sitting position as the man in *There's No Escape* did. Remember the instructions he had been given; go forward and roll on the floor as you imagine he would in the air.
    g. Work in groups, one to be the despatcher and the others the jumpers. Get in a line and imagine the opening to be just in front of the despatcher and at his side.
       Watch for the signal to jump, and move on his orders. Do it moving slowly forwards as if the plane were moving, so that you jump in different places.
5. Be a man on the ground watching a parachutist jump. Follow him with your eyes, quickly as he falls and more slowly as his parachute opens. Go over to help him to pull in the parachute when he has landed.
6. Join 3., 4., and 5. together.

Written work

(Most of the items in **The story of the horse** *could be used as the starting point for writing, much of which could come in verse.)*

1. Make up a story or poem as if you had been one of those who:
    a. Escaped from Troy.
    b. Entered the city.

   c. Were asleep in the town when the invaders arrived.
   d. Was the messenger to Diomed.
   e. Were left behind at the first camp.
   f. Were guarding the tower.
   g. Saw a friend killed in the fighting.
   h. Rescued a child.
   i. Saw a child crying for its dead parent.

(*The choice from these and other sections will indicate which parts of the movement/drama work have had the greatest impact on each child.*)

2. You were inside the horse with Odysseus. What was it like? Tell the story in your own way.
3. You were in the city when the horse was brought in. What might you have thought about it?
4. Tell the story as if you were a 'fed-up' soldier—'then there was work ...' ('The Spearman', from 'The Tale of Troy').
5. Write a song of the sacking of Troy on the lines of the 'War Song of Dinas Vawr'.
6. Masefield mentions a stringent watch being kept for any traitor. Why should a man become a traitor? Tell the story as though you were the traitor. Think of the way you had to act, the things you had to do, how you felt when you knew your attempts had failed.
7. Describe the scene when the trap-door opens. Think of the air rushing in, the noise, what you can see, and what you feel.
8. What thoughts would you think would be in a man's mind when he jumps with a parachute?
9. Describe what you think your impression would be of floating through the air like the pendulum of a clock.
10. Try to think of a new situation for the landing and describe what happened to you from the time the parachute opened.
11. Tell the story of a parachute jump as though you were the despatcher. Think how different men might look and act. What is it like when they have all gone?

Cowboys and Indians

It is interesting to wonder why the Western occupies such a prominent place in our children's enthusiasms. One can see the cowboy as an American folk hero, but why our pupils, with no such parallels in our culture, have taken him up so completely is much more mysterious. However, they certainly have and must often have a badly confused idea of what cowboys and Indians are. Colourful images of tall, silent men living by their guns, and feathered, half-naked, painted savages arise!

This theme lends itself to two kinds of development.

1. The fostering of creative work using the fantasies on which the 'Cowboy and Indian' myths are based.
2. The encouraging of inquiry into the true facts; the history of some of the Indian tribes and their locations; their present position in American life; the opening up of the American West, and so on. For the latter type of development a team teaching approach has much to recommend it.

Other elements which have emerged from the stories of the West—the stereotypes of the American cavalry, or the grizzly prospector, or events such as the coming of the railroad, for example—can be involved.

Readings

Panning for Gold	*When the Legends Die* Ch. 10	Hal Borland
First Rodeo	*When the Legends Die* Ch. 22	Hal Borland
Cowboys	*Man-shy* Ch. 4	Frank Dalby Davison
Branding	*Man-shy* Ch. 5	Frank Dalby Davison
The Diggings	*Bullwhip Griffin* Ch. 11	Sid Fleischman
	Red Indian Folk and Fairy Tales	Ruth Manning-Sanders
The Indians Attack	*Master Entrick* Ch.10, 15	Michael Mott
The Cowboy	*Shane* Ch. 1	Jack Schaefer
Shane rounds up the steers	*Shane* Ch. 5	Jack Schaefer
Shane shows Bob how to shoot	*Shane* Ch. 5	Jack Schaefer

Stampede	*Boss of the Namko Drive* Ch. 4	Paul St. Pierre
Days and Nights of Trial	*Nkwala: The Story of a Red Indian Boy*	Edith Sharp
The Indian Attack	*Children on the Oregon Trail* Ch. 2	A. Rutgers van der Loeff
	Red Indian Legends	ed. Louise Jean Walker
The Sioux Indians	Anon.	*Voices* 1
The American Indian	Anon.	*Voices* 2
Western Wagons	Stephen Vincent Benét	*Pegasus* 2
Jesse James	W. R. Benét	*Round the Day*
Cowboy Song	Charles Causley	*Voices* 2; *The Albemarle Book of Modern Verse* 1
The Flower-fed Buffaloes	Vachel Lindsay	*This Way Delight; Enjoying Poetry* 6
	H. W. Longfellow	*The Song of Hiawatha*
Cowboys	Jon Stallworthy	*Voices* 2
The Ox-Tamer	Walt Whitman	*Voices* 2

Movement/drama

General
Practise:
  a. Walking slowly like a cowboy setting up a camp for the night on the prairie.
  b. Tracking stealthily like a Red Indian.
  c. Sending smoke signals.
  d. Being a prospector, leading a mule, stopping to examine the rocks. Think of the heat and the glare.
  e. Panning for gold in a stream.
  f. Working in a group as a gang of rustlers, driving off horses or cows at night. Think how you are going to move and keep the animals quiet.
  Decide for yourselves whether you get away or not. If there is any trouble, show clearly what happens.

Cowboys
1. Train or break in a horse or an ox.

2. Drive a stage coach. Have a partner to ride beside you with a shotgun. Can you work out a mime where something happens? Remember to give it a beginning, a middle, and an end.

3. Ride a 'bucking bronco'. Hold on with one hand. Ride without hands. Be the horse, and buck and kick. Think particularly about your back and shoulders.

4. Stalk and chase Red Indians. Be sure of the path you are going to take, make detours, and don't be seen.

5. Jump off your horse onto a young bullock and hold it to the ground.

6. Throw your lassoo. Practise this. Can you do other imaginary tricks with a rope? Ride alongside and throw your lassoo over a steer. Draw it in to you.

7. Work in a group on cattle branding. Talk it over first to decide what you have to do and how you are going to cope with the cattle.

8. Can you work out a group mime of cowboys at a card game where something happens?

9. Feed and groom your horse; lead it over rocks; up a steep slope, down a steep slope; along the edge of a gorge; through a rocky ford in a river (remember you will have to coax and urge it to do the things you want it to do).
Get it to stand and keep quiet while you creep away to watch something. It goes lame while you are riding. Examine your horse and show what you are going to do.
Ride it, hear a shot, roll off, and take cover. Signal to your horse and get it out of the way.

10. Practise a quick draw and shot. Do it in different situations: walking along and hearing a shot from the rear; facing someone; while running to a noise. Try trick shooting of all kinds at moving targets; from different positions (looking in a mirror, over your shoulder, etc.).

Indians

1. Track and shoot with a bow and arrow.
2. Ride furiously with spears waving.
3. Examine tracks in the dust.
4. Skin an animal. Scrape and dress the skins.
5. Paint your body and face, and prepare for battle.
6. Ride into battle and get shot. What happens to you?
7. Work with a partner. He is a paleface asleep, you a Red Indian.
You creep up on him. He starts, wakens, and moves away. He speaks but you do not understand and answer in your own language (which you

make up). Carry on a conversation where the tone of your voice will give indications of what you are thinking. Change over.

8. Go canoeing. Read 'Hiawatha's Sailing' (*Song of Hiawatha*, Chapter 7). Make your canoe, launch it, and take it down the river. Think of the different things you will have to do in the river (avoiding snags or floating objects). Try shooting the rapids.

9. Have an Indian dance. (*Music:* Gayane *by Khachaturyan*). Read about the dance of Pau-Puk-Keewis at Hiawatha's wedding (*Song of Hiawatha*, Chapter 11).

Listen to the music.

Make up a dance of your own on the spot. Try to remember to alter the height, path, and speed of your movements. Don't be afraid to be still and hold a position.

Move about the room now as you dance.

Some be watchers and some dancers. Let the watchers beat out the time and try to react to the dancers.

Group drama

Rodeo

This can be developed from the individual practices in **Cowboys**. The rodeo will include galloping, trick horsemanship, bucking bronco riding, lassooing, trick shooting, roping steers. Children can work in groups or individually (as in the development of the **Circus** theme.)

The attack

A possible sequence would be:

Waggon train sets up camp for the night, watched by Indian scouts.

Travellers settle down, leaving a few guards.

Indians creep up.

One man killed by arrow alerts guards.

Settlers rush to positions while Indians circle camp.

Fierce fighting, many dead and wounded, wives and children assist settlers, Indians setting fire to waggons, etc.

Trumpet blast. Arrival of cavalrymen who begin to fire on Indians. Attack driven off, settlers care for wounded, etc.

Indians withdraw, and have a council of war.

(Alternatives include a truce, an ambush, or an Indian victory.)

Hiawatha

Groups or class mimes can be applied to almost any chapters of *The Song of Hiawatha.*

Written work

1. You are an Indian boy or girl. What sort of things do you have to learn?
2. Before a boy becomes a brave, he has to pass a test to prove his bravery and manhood. You are an Indian boy; what do you have to do? Describe how you take the test and what happens. (Read 'Days and Nights of Trial' from *Nkwala: The Story of a Red Indian Boy*, by Edith Sharp.)
3. Write a description of a cowboy who rode onto your ranch.
4. Write an imaginary account of an Indian attack on a stage coach as seen by an Indian or a passenger.
5. You are a settler's child, and you are friends with an old Indian. Tell about your friendship, where you meet, what he is like, and the things you do together.
6. Write a vivid account of a round-up or cattle drive.
7. Describe a western township. Give it a name and imagine you have just ridden into it after a long trail.
8. As realistically as you can, write an imagined account of a day on the trail. Decide first what jobs you have to do.
9. Imagine you are a waggon master. Tell about one of your journeys.
10. Tell such a story as Iagoo, the great boaster, might have told at Hiawatha's wedding.
11. Which is your favourite T.V. or film western character? Describe him.
12. Suppose you were an Indian; tell about the coming of the white man to your land and all it meant to you.
13. A children's skipping rhyme starts 'Cowboy Joe from Mexico ...' Can you continue this in a rhyme of your own?
14. Why do you think the buffalo was so important to the Indians? Write as though you were an Indian chief who found the buffalo disappearing from his hunting frounds.
15. Write a character sketch of any typical character from a Western: 'the cook', 'the gambler', 'the saloon keeper', 'the old scout', 'the cavalry sergeant', 'the baddy'.

Witches and Spells

From very early years children will meet witches in fairy stories and legends, and they will have a very generalized image of a witch. They will certainly get a great deal of pleasure from this as a theme, and at the same time it affords certain special opportunities.

The first of these is in spoken and written language. I wrote in Part I of how children should be encouraged to experiment with intonation and stress in words. Repeating a witch's spell to give different emphasis, perhaps on words that are not so obviously important at first, and to produce different patterns of sound, is a good example. Such experiments add strength to the movement activities and other expressive forms. The evocative use of written language should be stimulated by plentry of discussion about words with 'witch-like' qualities, stressing the nature of the sound and how this can be emphasized in the writing.

The other great function of this work should be developing the awareness of small body parts and the role each plays in a complete portrait. Examples of this are given in the movement/drama exercises. Others will arise as teachers watch their children and analyse responses.

Readings

	The Hamish Hamilton Book of Witches	(ed.) J. Hope-Simpson
	Witches, witches, witches	(ed.) Helen Hoke
	Journey by Broomstick	(ed.) G. Palmer and N. Lloyd
Witches' Spells	*Weirdstone of Brisingamen* Ch. 9	Alan Garner
Granny Billing's Spell	*The Hungry Cloud* Ch. 13	Tom Ingram
Dinah's Spell	*The Wind on the Moon* Ch. 5	Eric Linklater
Miss Price on the Broomstick	*The Magic Bed-knob* Ch. 1, 2, 3	Mary Norton

Miss Price in her Workshop	*The Magic Bed-knob* Ch. 1, 2, 3	Mary Norton
The Woman	*The Cold Flame* Ch. 3	James Reeves
Getting Rid of Warts	*The Adventures of Tom Sawyer* Ch. 6	Mark Twain
Madame Nim	*The Sword in the Stone* Ch. 6	T. H. White
Witches' Song and Spell	*The Sword in the Stone* Ch. 6	T. H. White
Duel between Merlin and Madame Nim	*The Sword in the Stone* Ch. 6	T. H. White
Good Wish	Anon.	*The Faber Book of Children's Verse*
Charms	Anon.	*Junior Voices* 1
Four Charms	Anon.	*Junior Voices* 2
A Country Witch	W. Barnes	*The Golden Treasury of Poetry*
The Witch	Mary Coleridge	*The Oxford Book of Verse for Juniors* 3
hist whist	e. e. cummings	*The Merry-Go-Round*
The Ride-by-Nights	Walter de la Mare	*The Oxford Book of Verse for Juniors* 3; *Poetry and Life* 3; *The Merry-Go-Round; Mood and Rhythm* 1
I saw Three Witches	Walter de la Mare	*The Oxford Book of Verse for Juniors* 3
W is for Witch	Eleanor Farjeon	*The Children's Bells*
The Two Witches	Robert Graves	*Happenings* 1; *Dawn and Dusk; Voices* 1
The Hag	Robert Herrick	*The Faber Book of Children's Verse; Common Ground; The Oxford Book of Poetry for Children; Mood and Rhythm* 3; *Voices* 1; *My Kind of Verse*
The Witch	Percy H. Ilott	*The Book of a Thousand Poems*
Witches' Charm	Ben Jonson	*The Merry-Go-Round; The Oxford Book of Poetry for Children; This Way Delight*

Space Travellers	James Nimmo	*The Oxford Book of Verse for Juniors* 3; *Poetry and Life* 4; *Birthright Poetry* 2; *Poetry Panorama* 3
Spells	James Reeves	*All Day Long; My Kind of Verse; Birthright Poetry* 2; *A Puffin Quartet of Poets; Exploring Poetry* 3
The Witch's Cat	Ian Serraillier	*Happenings* 1; *Happily Ever After*
Three Witches	William Shakespeare	*Macbeth,* Act IV, Sc. I.
A Witch's Chant	J. Wilson	*Rhyme and Rhythm* (blue)

Movement/drama

Use parts of your body as you think a witch would:
1. *a. Hands.* Close your eyes and see a witch's hand in front of you.
    Examine it carefully until you are sure you know what it is like.
    Think about the shape of the fingers, the nails, knuckles, lines,
    veins, and so on.
    Hold up your own hand in front of you and watch it change into a
    witch's hand. Do it slowly and feel your hand change. Feel your
    changed hand with the other one, and vice versa.
    Turn it over and watch the other side.
    Do it with both hands at the same time.
  Use your witch's hand to:
  a. Grip something.
  b. Twist something.
  c. Stroke a wall, the floor, an animal.
  d. Let something run through your fingers.
  e. Reach out for something.
  f. Point and follow the movement of something.
  g. Beckon to something as though you wanted it to come to you or
    go away. Combine these two.
  h. Rub your hands together.
  i. Arrange small things in different piles. Think how you are going to
    hold the different things.

j. Prepare some things (plants, animals) for spells.

k. Use your hand to fashion a spell.

2. *Face.* Close your eyes and see a witch's face in front of you. Hold an imaginary mirror up to your face and see it slowly change into a witch's face. Which parts of your face can you alter? Think particularly about these parts. Change your face so that you are a witch—plotting, suspicious, angry, greedy, gleeful, leering. Go back over some of the things you did in 1. above and this time try to make your hands and face movements fit together to show the mood you are in. Alter the mood; for example, you could be suspicious, catch and twist something, then be happy.

3. *Arms and Body.* Practise:

    a. Wrapping your cloak about your body.

    b. Stirring a cauldron.

    c. Preparing to ride a broomstick.

    d. Running through a wood. Make the sound you think a witch might before you begin.

        Try different sounds—rushing, short, sharp, etc.

        Try as many different sounds as you can and make your movements fit them.

    e. Creep up to something.

    f. Make a trap and then wait for something to be caught.

    g. Wait for your captive. Think how you are going to handle it. Examine your captives in their cages dotted about the hall. Think how you are going to move from one to another. Try to show your feelings as you move and examine your captives.

    h. Call all the other witches to a meeting. Work with a group of about six. Talk it over first and decide what you will do, who is going to call you together, the positions you are going to be in before you are called, what you are going to do when you come together, and what sort of group you are going to make.

    i. Act a scene about making a spell. Use all your body and move freely as you do it.

    If written work has been done before this, it should be incorporated with the movement/drama so that the children are moving to their own spells or in groups to other children's. If not, 'gibberish' sounds to fit the movements could be made to encourage extremes of movement, and these patterns of sound repeated, or the teacher could read a spell, usually in couplets, and get a movement response from the children. By altering the speed and phrasing, great variety is possible here.

Class/drama

Macbeth (Act IV, Scene 1)

1. Before beginning the children should have heard this piece many times, have talked about it, had an opportunity to read it aloud and to themselves, perhaps have done some choral speaking with it, and later will need to memorize certain parts of it.
2. In order to really explore the extract in terms of movement and speech, the build-up to the finished product should be very gradual and, before the final selection of parts by the children themselves, they should have experience in all parts. Initially, the order of activities is of no importance. The use of percussion and music could add a great deal to the feeling of the piece. Normal techniques of children watching each other and working in different groupings apply. A possible sequence could be:

1. Practise coming into the cave as though you were a witch. (*Thunder Sounds*) What ways could you come in? Explode, creep, rush, sidle, etc.
2. Practise throwing poisoned entrails into the pot. Try to make a little sequence so you collect, do something, throw, do something, etc.
3. Practise movements to the chorus lines. Learn the lines first and say them in as many ways as you can.

Teacher can make different emphases and perhaps extend the lines herself to open up possibilities. This should be class work where one person (teacher or child) says lines and all children move individually, then group work where first one group speaks and the other group moves; then one person speaks and the group move to him; and finally the group speak and move together. After these practices, children should establish their way of moving and speaking before continuing to the next part.

4. Teacher reads first witch's speech and children move to it. This should be done several times with the teacher altering ways of speaking and all children responding to it individually, and all ending with the chorus which has already been learned and practised. This should then be extended to other speeches on the same lines. For example:

      First witch—one voice—all move

      Chorus—own voices—all move

      Second witch—one voice—all move

      Chorus—own voices—all move

Then children can be asked to be just one witch and move as their lines are spoken, still responding to the previously practised chorus lines for all. Next, children speak and move to the lines they have picked, still moving individually with teacher or child calling out when speeches begin. Then speak and move consecutively still as a class of individuals. Finally group work with each child having one part to play in the group and each group working separately in their own time and space.

The Sword in the Stone

1. Make a list of the things which Merlin and Madame Nim turn themselves into.

   Pick out one thing from the list and make your body shape into that shape. Try as many ways as you can, and find your best shape. From it move into the second shape you have picked from the list. Try to get a good way of joining them together. Practise moving from your first shape to your second.

   Take a third shape and work out a pattern of movement from your first to your second to your third shape. Make your shapes clear and repeat them until you know your pattern.

2. Work with a partner. Let your partner make any shape with his body and you copy it. Watch him carefully and try to do exactly as he has done. Change over and then work in sequence, each copying the other in turn.

3. Arrange your partner's body in any shape you like. Pick one he can hold comfortably.

   a. Be a painter and paint him as he is arranged.
   b. Be a sculptor and model his body in that shape.
   c. Be a photographer and take snaps of his shape from all positions.
   d. Now put your body into his shape *exactly.*

4. Work with a partner and try to get the opposite shape from his; if he is small and round, you make yourself big and jagged, and so on. Look at all parts of his shape first and get yours unlike his in every respect. Speed this up with every shape getting a different response. Change the leader. Now with your partner work out a pattern of different opposite shapes, each with a good joining movement. Try to vary the shape, speed, and height of your movements. Practise this form of dance until you are sure of it.

5. Now move round the hall any way you like. At the signal, respond in any way you like to the shape that the person next to you makes. When you meet someone next time, each do something, then respond to the other person's shape and movement. You may do it together or one after the other. (*Some music or sounds here will be of great help*). Carry on doing this with anyone you meet.

6. Arrange yourselves in groups to act out Madame Nim's contest with Merlin. Have a timekeeper or referee and at least two spectators. Talk over your sequence before you begin and devise some music signals for the changes. Remember you all have a part to play and respond all the time.

Written work

1. Make up a poem of spells or charms. Think what you want to happen first.
2. In olden times witches were blamed for all sorts of things. Has anything ever happened to you that you would like to blame a witch for?
3. Write a poem about a particular part of a witch's body.
4. What do you think witches talk about when they meet? Write about a witches' meeting.
5. Write a song like Madame Nim's when she was preparing her meal. Think how you examined all your captives in their cages. Tell about it. Don't be afraid to make up strange words.
6. Tell what happened to you one very unquiet night when you heard a strange noise, got up out of bed, and looked out of the window ...
7. Describe a witch's house, cave, or workshop.
8. Imagine you were watching the three Macbeth witches in the cavern. Tell the story of what happened and how you felt.
9. Why should all witches seem bad? Make up a spell that a good witch might use or tell the story of a happy witch.
10. In *The Magic Bedknob*, Miss Price was quite a harmless looking person, with perhaps just a little mystery about her. Tell how you found out that she was a witch.

Mysteries

This is a theme capable of wide interpretation by both teachers and children, with a natural appeal to all ages. To some extent it involves fantasy by presenting a field of exploration which is outside the child's everyday experience but which can be firmly rooted in the imagination. The work needs little external motivation, and the degree of identification which the child achieves should be very high. With many children the exploration of the extraordinary will naturally be a rigorous intellectual exercise. However, in the writing the teacher must guard against imprecise and automatic responses from the children. These can be avoided by discussion, by helping the children define the point of view which they want to express, and by getting them to work for authenticity of detail and feeling. Dramatic work, quite apart from its intrinsic value, is especially useful in establishing such authenticity.

Readings

The Triangle	*Travelling Magic* Ch. 2	Elizabeth Beresford
Mary Enters the Garden	*The Secret Garden* Ch.8 (also in *Thoughtshapes*)	Frances Hodgson Burnett
Strange Evening at Home	*Elidor* Ch. 10	Alan Garner
Mole in the Wild Wood	*The Wind in the Willows* Ch. 3	Kenneth Grahame
Calling the Porpoises	*A Pattern of Islands* Ch. 6	Sir Arthur Grimble
What Happened about the Statues	*The Lion, the Witch, and the Wardrobe* Ch.16	C. S. Lewis
In the Garden	*Tom's Midnight Garden* Ch. 2, 3, 5	Philippa Pearce
The Piper	*Brother Dusty-Feet* Ch. 4	Rosemary Sutcliff

Mr. Nobody	Anon.	*Poetry and Life* 2; *The Merry-Go-Round; The Book of a Thousand Poems*
The Pied Piper of Hamelin	R. Browning	*Birthright Poetry* 3; *The Faber Book of Children's Verse; The Golden Treasury*
Jabberwocky	Lewis Carroll	*Rhyme and Rhythm* (yellow); *Voices* 1; *Birthright Poetry* 4
The Deserted House	Mary Coleridge	*This Way Delight; Come Hither; The Book of a Thousand Poems; The Merry-Go-Round; Thought-shapes*
Kubla Khan	Samuel Taylor Coleridge	*This Way Delight; The Faber Book of Children's Verse; The Golden Journey; Iron, Honey, Gold* 2; *Other Men's Flowers*
The Vacant Farmhouse	Walter de la Mare	*The Harrap Book of Modern Verse*
The Listeners	Walter de la Mare	*Poetry and Life* 4; *The Pilgrim Book of Verse* 2; *This Way Delight; Birthright Poetry* 4
I know some Lonely Houses off the Road	Emily Dickinson	*Iron, Honey, Gold* 2; *Junior Voices* 3
Flannan Isle	Wilfrid Gibson	*The Pilgrim Book of Verse* 2; *Come Hither; Mood and Rhythm* 2; *Enjoying Poetry* 2; *The Oxford Book of Poetry for Children*
The Old Wife and the Ghost	James Reeves	*Blackwell's Junior Poetry Book* 3; *Poetry and Life* 2

I Mystery at sea

Movement/drama

Flannan Isle

1. Close your eyes. You are in the empty lighthouse. What sounds can you hear? (Birds, sea, wind, creaking doors.)

   Pick out just one of the sounds and listen to that. Can you smell anything (sea, wood, tar, food)? Try to get one smell fixed in your mind. You have to investigate one of the sounds or smells. When you are ready, move off to find out about it. Show what happens.

2. Sit on the floor. Look around the room. You see some strange birds. Keep your eyes fixed on them as they move. Show what happens when:

      they are coming closer and closer to you

      they are circling and going away.

   Get up into a position for watching the birds and moving towards them. Do they move too? Try to get as near as you can to the birds. Have they anything special about them. Do you feel anything special coming from them Do they affect you in any way? (Your eyes!) How do they go away?

3. Move as the men would (think how they are feeling and let your movements show what is in your mind):

   a. Watching the 'blinded lantern' from the ship.

   b. Climbing the track to the lighthouse.

   c. Coming to the door left open.

   d. Plucking up courage to open it and go into the living-room. What do you see now? How are you going to move?

   e. Opening another door. Practise many ways of doing this.

   f. Ransacking the empty house and searching from shore to shore of the island. Think how your movements are going to alter as you search. Also remember you are working in different positions on different types of ground. A bang on the cymbal means a noise disturbs you while you search. Show what happens.

4. Put your body into a 'rock' shape, try to make as many 'crannies, clefts, or nooks' as you can. Try several shapes until you get the best.

   Work with a partner. One is the rock and the other the searcher, who approaches the rock and examines it. Change the rock shape, and try again.

   Let part of the rock fall down or move. What happens? Change over parts. In a group try to arrange yourselves as an interesting collection of rocks. Think about the different heights (use apparatus if you want to), shapes, spaces, tunnels, holes, etc. Let one person search amongst these rocks.

5. Be the three men on the island. You are getting ready for a meal when

something happens. Talk it over first to decide what might happen to make you leave your meal. There are many strange things that could happen and many ways you could go. Try to work out some order of events which will leave the room empty. You could work at several plans before deciding which is best. Is there to be a sound made? It might help at the beginning.

Written work

1. Tell the story as though you were one of the men who disappeared.
2. How did you feel when you saw 'the black, sun-blistered light-house' door.
3. You are a newspaper reporter. Write an account for your paper of the strange happenings on Flannan Isle and the story the three men who came back told. You might have an exclusive interview with one of them or with a relative of a missing man.
4. Do you think the three men were dead? Can you think of an ending to the story beginning

> Three men alive on Flannan Isle
> Who thought on three men dead ... ?

5. Describe the island as in a travel brochure.
6. Write a story telling about the lives of the men who died on Flannan Isle during their last few hours.

II Mysterious houses

Movement/drama

1. Shut your eyes.
   a. Listen to a clock striking: one, two ... thirteen!
   b. Listen to the stillness of the room.
   c. Touch your face with the tips of your fingers as slowly and lightly as you can. How does it feel? Feel your face all over with your finger-tips very lightly.
   d. Reach out with your hands and feel an imaginary object. Do it with something small; something large; things of your own choice.
   e. Feel the floor with your toes.
   f. Lift one foot. Stroke your other leg with it as lightly as possible.
   g. Reach out and put your hands into different things—a pot of sticky glue; a sack of feathers; a cold slimy pool; on to a damp wall. Show how the touch of your hands on these things affects you.

2. Look into a far corner of the room, keep your eyes fixed there, and as the cymbal roll increases, see a face appear. Turn to look somewhere else. Can you see a different face this time? Can you make the shadows on the wall or floor into a face? Look at a wall and pick out all the patterns you can. Make these into something.

3. You are staying in a strange house. Set out to explore a dark corridor. You come to a door, find a key, and open it. Show what happens.

4. Move as you would in a deserted house.

   a. Brush a cobweb from your face.
   b. Try to look through a window that is blackened by time.
   c. Lift up a rusted trapdoor.
   d. Sort out what is left in an old cupboard.
   e. Examine a pile of old books.
   f. Make your way across a deserted garden.
   g. Try to make some part of the garden more presentable like Mary did in *The Secret Garden*.
   h. Put some of these things together and develop a mime of going into such a house.

5. Move as Tom did when he got up in the night and found the midnight garden. Can you see it? Be Tom moving as he thought he would next day: running full tilt over the grass, leaping the flower beds, peering through, the greenhouse panes, etc. Be Tom seeing the maid approaching. Act through this scene. Can you see things changing? Try to concentrate on an imaginary object and watch it as it disappears or changes to something else. Make sure you know what it is. Continue the scene of Tom and the maid. See the room change back again when the maid disappears. Really watch it and show how you feel. Make sure you know what is going to happen before you begin.

6. Take up a position to be one of the 'phantom listeners' in 'The Listeners'. Move as you would when you hear the music. (*Music: Ghost-like quality* – Night on a Bare Mountain *by Mussorgsky*; Pavane pour une infante défunte *by Ravel*). Try different ways of moving to this music, holding your position from time to time. You can work out a dance sequence. A tap on the drum is the traveller knocking at the door. Show what happens now as you listen and watch him. The 'sound of iron on stone' lets you continue with your movement, though differently. Why is it different?

   Let there now be some travellers who say the spoken lines from 'The Listeners' and the others play their parts as listeners.

Written work

1. Listen again to Philippa Pearce's description of the time very early in the morning, before anything is awake. Write a piece about that time.
2. How does she describe dawn coming in *Tom's Midnight Garden*? Write a description yourself.
3. You were Tom, Marcus, or Kate. Tell the story of what happened (*Tom's Midnight Garden*).
4. Have you ever seen something that no one else saw? Tell about it.
5. Do things ever look different to you? Perhaps ordinary things do at certain times.
6. Which is the strangest house or building you have ever seen?
7. Write the story of 'The Listeners' as though you had been either the traveller or one of the phantoms.
8. Write a poem about ghosts. Try to give it a shape on the page to help the feeling.
9. Tell the story of your night in the strange house.

III Mystery at home

Movement/drama

1. Sit on the floor. You are at home by the fire and you hear a tapping on the window. Listen to it. Pluck up your courage and go to draw back the curtains. Find nothing and settle down again. Hear the tapping repeated, work out an ending, and show what happens. (You might see a face this time).
2. Be a ghost. Move as it would coming into the kitchen. See some mischief to be done and do it.
   Add a ghost-like sound to your movement.
   When you hear the signal it means the Old Wife ('The Old Wife and The Ghost') has stirred in her sleep. What are you going to do now? Work in a group of three or four as ghosts in the kitchen. Work out a sequence of events which will have times when just one of you will move and times when you are all moving. How are you going to enter and leave the room? Can you add a part for the Old Wife to this scene?
3. *a.* Tune an imaginary T.V. set, fiddle with the controls to get a picture. Work with a partner, one to do the adjusting, the other to watch the picture and give instructions. Think how you will feel as the picture gets no better, and speak about it.
   b. You have a small clockwork toy which won't go. Try to mend it.

    c. Your toy won't stop; try to stop it.

    d. Be a clockwork toy. When you hear the music, start with just one part of your body working (e.g. perhaps your head); bring in other parts until it is all going. Try from different starting positions. Practise on the spot before you move about the floor. Make your movements jerky. Think how you are going to turn and what your path is to be on the floor.

    Go through this again when you know your best sequence.

    This time let the toy break down so that one part keeps repeating and the sequence is broken. Work with a partner. Let the partner try to mend the toy. Does it work now? Change over.

    Go through a sequence and let your partner try to stop you.

4. Work in a group and make up a comic sketch entitled 'The Haunted House'.

Written work

1. Tell the story as though you were the Old Wife.
2. Have you a 'Mr. Nobody' in your home? What does he do that you get blamed for?
3. Can you think of any explanation for the mysterious happenings in *Elidor*?
4. Tell the story of the face you saw at the window.
5. Tell the story of anything strange that has happened at your home.
6. Describe an evening at home when *everything* went wrong.

IV Mysteries with animals

Movement/drama

Mole in the Wild Wood

1. Sit down and shut your eyes. Something is watching you from behind. Can you feel its eyes boring into you? A tap on the drum means it touches you. What happens then? Let it touch you in different ways (not always frightening), and on different parts of your body. Feel it now on your own without the drum tap. Turn quickly when you feel it is right up to you.

    From where you are, look round the room and see faces looking at you from odd places. Really look at them.

2. Make a 'hard-eyed, evil, sharp face' yourself. Try different ways. Can you make it just with your eyes, or mouth, or both?

Get into a position for watching someone move through the wood. Watch him, show your face, and disappear. Move away so that you will see him again and make your face again, then disappear.

Keep on doing this from different positions.

3. Move as Mole would:
    a. Going into the Wild Wood. Stop to look at things and show how you are feeling. Let the going get a bit harder as you go deeper into the wood.
    b. Feeling that a face is watching him. Go to a bush or tree, part the branches carefully, and look for the face. Move along as he did after his first encounter. What are you telling yourself?

4. Work in groups of half a dozen or so. One be Mole and the others the faces. Watch Mole as he travels and make your faces at him. Make sure you use all the space you have and work out first where he is going to see you. Try to get it so that the 'faces' move about as Mole goes along and finish up so that you are all around him, coming and going so that he has to flee away in panic. What will the faces do then?

5. Practise making a strange noise. It may be a whistling, hissing, eerie, frightening noise. Make it to yourself first, work at altering its speed and pitch until you have a pattern. Work with a partner, one sit down and close your eyes, the other creep up and make your noise so that only your partner can hear it. Change over.

    One person sit and listen to a group making their own noises. Try to pick out just one and listen to that.

6. Make a pattering noise with any part of your body. Fingers, hands, feet, tongue, lips. Make this into a rhythm that gets louder. Practise until you are sure you get a good pattern.

7. Put 5. and 6. together. Some be Moles just hearing the first noises and turning to them. When you get the signal change from the whistling to the pattering and watch Mole as he finally moves in panic, until he struggles down into the safe hollow. What is going to happen to the 'noise makers' then? Work as a class with a few Moles.

8. In groups now can you work out a sequence for the whole scene? You will have to play more than one part.

Written work

1. Tell the story as though you were one of the wicked faces.
2. Be Mole and describe your adventure in the Wild Wood.
3. Have you ever felt that something was watching you? Tell about it.
4. Make up a humorous ending to the story.

Movement/drama

The Pied Piper of Hamelin

1. Be the Mayor before the rat epidemic began. Put on your fine ermine cloak and costume, showing what it means to you, and walk around the town as he would. What sort of things might he do?

2. Be the people of the town. Decide what you are: shopkeepers, sweepers, gossipers, mothers, children. Show what you would do as the Mayor goes round (before the plague).
   Some be Mayors and others townspeople. The Mayors move around while the others are working. React to each other.

3. Now we have one Mayor moving through the town amongst the angry people. How are they going to react to him *now*? Let the action continue with the Mayor making his way to the Council Chamber, the people gathering about the door, and continuing their parts after he goes in.

4. Inside the Council Chamber. Can you work out a scene where the Mayor and Council are discussing this problem, while the crowd outside finally elect some representatives to make their demands? Use either the poet's or your own words.

5. All be the Pied Piper. Walk through the town.
   Now work in groups to be people who see the Pied Piper. How are they going to respond to this strange character? Now, have one Pied Piper and the rest in groups as townspeople. Set up the Council Chamber scene again with the people dispersed outside: see the Piper come into town, and go into the Council Chamber; and listen while he and the Mayor come to their agreement. Do you think they all believe the Pied Piper can do as he says?

6. All be Pied Pipers charming the rats away.
   All be the townspeople seeing the rats go. Think how you felt before.
   All be Mayors watching the success.
   Work at this in groups.
   Split up again so that we have a class scene with one Mayor, one Piper, city councillors, and townspeople. Don't be the same as you were before. Take your scene to be the time when the Pied Piper goes back to the Council Chamber and the Mayor refuses to pay him. (*Music and percussion signals*).

7. Be children playing in the street or at home.
   Hear strange music and be drawn towards it. Try this as many ways as you can from different starting positions with a different response.
   Be parents doing something and then seeing their children go. What are you going to do?

Be a lame boy trying to catch up with the rest. See your friends disappear, and return to the town.

Be the townspeople. Watch the children finally go. Move as you think they would after the children disappear. You might want to work with a partner or a small group. Can you give the feeling of the town at this time, by your movements or by the positions you take up? In your final positions, watch as the lame boy comes back and goes to the Council Chamber. All should now be still.

8. You can now put it all together into a class play. You will need a Mayor, a Pied Piper, parents, councillors, children, and a lame boy. Your teacher will give you music or percussion signals for the scenes to begin. Remember to end very quietly and still, with perhaps just the lame boy moving back into town with the parents watching him.

Written work

1. You are the Pied Piper. Make up a story about some other deed you did before you came to Hamelin.
2. Tell the story of the town getting plagued with rats as if you lived there. (*Teacher might like to read passages from the early part of* The Plague by *Albert Camus*).
3. What steps do you think they took to get rid of the rats?
4. Write a poem about the feeling of the town when the rats had gone.
5. Listen again to what Robert Browning said about the rats ('Rats, rats, . . .') Can you make up a poem about rats?
6. Tell what happened to you as one of the children.
7. What do you think the town was like when the children had gone? Write about it.
8. Do you believe this poem? Who was the Pied Piper? Why do you think Browning wrote it? Write what you think about it.

Calling the Porpoises

This also gives opportunities for the development of a class drama. Again the children should be given experiences in all the parts involved while the drama is gradually brought together as a whole. This extract also gives plenty of scope for extensions such as tribal dances, feast scenes, primitive mystery, which are independent of the script while still keeping within its field of feeling. Similarly the passages from *The Lion, the Witch, and the Wardrobe* and *Brother Dusty-Feet* have much to offer for individual and group practices.

Written work

1. Tell about the porpoises as if you had been there.
2. Make up a call or a prayer that the 'dreamer' might have said. Remember he had great respect for the porpoises.
3. Why do you think Sir Arthur Grimble 'rushed helter skelter and bawled at the top of his voice'? Have you ever been caught in this feeling of others doing something and having to join in? Tell about it.
4. Imagine you were the 'dreamer'. Tell about what happened in the hut.

Strange Creatures

As a result of comics and television, children are very aware of the world of science fiction and the strange creatures it spawns. How seriously they take these fantasies is open to question but one wonders if there is not now some confusion between the world of Apollo and the world of Dr. Who!

Though children are interested and often knowledgeable, their writing on this subject can be very superficial. They pick up the clichés of the mass media, though these may not be clichés to the children, string them together, and produce results lacking the involvement and creativity we are striving for. The real need is for a disciplined expression limiting the degree of technicality and verbal extravagance. This probably means that the fiction rather than the science must be stressed. Any suspension of belief required must be indicative of the child's imagination rather than the technical powers of the mass media at work.

The extent of the possible readings is large. I have kept this list short to highlight the possibilities of this theme and to show what I consider to be the best. I doubt if there is another field in which so much rubbish has been written, so great care is necessary in selection.

Readings

	The Iron Man	Ted Hughes
	The War of the Worlds (Beginning)	H. G. Wells
Village Cut off	*The Midwich Cuckoos* Ch. 1	John Wyndham
Arrival of the Sea Tanks	*The Kraken Wakes* Phase 2	John Wyndham
Space Pilot	J. Blackie	*Mystery, Magic, and Adventure*
Warning to Children	Robert Graves	*The Faber Book of Children's Verse; The Oxford Book of Poetry for Children; A Flock of Words*

Welsh Incident	Robert Graves	*Common Ground; Voices* 2; *The Albemarle Book of Modern Verse* 1; *Selected Poems; Pegasus* 4; *Harrap's Junior Book of Modern Verse; Penguin Book of Contemporary Verse*
Tea in a Space-Ship	James Kirkup	*Round the Day; The Albemarle Book of Modern Verse* 1
Space Travellers	James Nimmo	*The Oxford Book of Verse for Juniors* 3; *Poetry and Life* 4; *Birthright Poetry* 2; *Poetry Panorama* 4

Movement/drama

General

1. You are walking along and you find a crater in the ground. Show how you would react? Does anything move while you are there? Show what happens.
2. You are walking along and hear a sudden noise (*cymbal, drum*). Show your reaction.

   (*By varying the noise the teacher can evoke different responses. Some possibilities are:*
   sudden movement
   wonder leading to sudden movement
   repeated wonder, leading to climax
   nothing happens as a climax, and so on.)

3. You are a cameraman, either for stills or movies. Move about taking the best pictures you can of anything happening. Think of the angles of your photographs, the speed of your movements, and the method of your approach.
4. You are a scientist working on a formula for making people invisible. Practise mixing the formula and taking it. Show yourself:
   a. Failing to grow invisible. Think about your period of waiting and testing. Think how you would feel and react.

    b. Succeeding. How does it affect you? Does one part of your body feel strange first? Does the feeling spread? Does it affect your movements? Perhaps it makes you feel lighter? Could you think of a test for this? Can animals see you or are they aware you are there? How do you know you are invisible?

    c. Mix the potion to restore yourself. Do you succeed the first time? How do you feel now? Show your reactions as the feeling passes through all parts of your body.

    d. Work in pairs, one person to mix the potion and become invisible, the other to enter the room being certain the first person is there. Talk about how you are both going to react and act it out several times. Change places and re-act the scene.

5. Build yourself a space ship. You have all the materials you need around you in the hall. Fetch them from their different places as you build. Show by your movements what sort of materials you are using. They are:

    heavy (you pull, push, lift, or roll)

    light (you load, and control)

    large (you guide and control)

    small and delicate (these need most careful handling and installation)

    dangerous (these are capable of blowing up as you carry them)

Build your ship, and move round, under, and above it as you work. Introduce noises as you work.

Get a partner and explain to him all about the space machine you have made. Take him around and under it as you explain.

6. Break up your machine.

Break up your partner's machine while he breaks up yours.

7. Try walking through an invisible barrier. Think how it might slow you up, drag you down, engulf you, affect different parts of your body (eyes, feet, arms, chest), finally dragging you down to sleep.

Welsh Incident

1. Move as you think one of the creatures would. Vary your movements.

    a. Alter your height.

    b. Is the speed to be regular or irregular?

    c. Is the path to be straight or jerky?

    d. Which part of your body is leading the way or bearing the weight? Try different parts.

(After practice with these points in mind the children should practise the movement they find most rewarding and concentrate on that.)

2. 'Did something recognizably a something'. What might this be—a noise?
   Practise making noises with a movement to match. Try several different
   noises until you are sure you have the best to go with your movement.

   Any percussion instrument might help initially but the children ought
   to make their own noises. At first these will probably be loud and
   inflationary, but with the teacher pointing out the possibilities they
   should become varied.
   Electronic Sound Pattern recordings fit in well. Varied movements
   to them should be practised, freely at first, and then directed towards
   the theme.

3. Go back to the beginning of the poem, and practise the whole sequence
   of events, moving and adding the 'something' you did before.
4. Practise being:
   a. Bandsmen playing different instruments, first moving, then standing
      still.
   b. The conductor of the band.
   c. The Mayor, or important guests.
   d. Audience. Get a good starting position. Was the awareness immediate,
      or slowly dawning? Were you curious, afraid, or amused? (It might
      have been a prank.) Let your movements show your feelings. Change
      them and go from one feeling to another (i.e. from curious to afraid,
      amused to curious, and so on). Did you keep the same feeling through-
      out?
5. Work in pairs. Both have clear starting positions, one make the noise,
   and the other respond to it. Vary the noise and try to get the response
   to match it. Try to develop a simple pattern of noise and response.
   Change over.

   After practise in these parts by the children, this should now be built
   up into a class drama with different groups of children acting out the
   different parts in the hall or gym. It will not be a single production
   (i.e. there need not be one group of bandsmen or one group of 'things'
   coming from the same place, rather there will be several of each with
   children alternating parts). Finally it could develop into a single whole
   with perhaps a link provided by two people playing the obvious speaking parts, in their own or the poet's language.

The Kraken Wakes

1. All practise being pulled along. Show which part of your body has been
   caught by the scilla. Do you resist all the time? Practise different
   positions for your resistance and make sure you have a clear position
   for the start. Vary the part of your body being pulled; be aware of which

part of your body is leading the way. Is the speed even and the path straight? What happens when you try to brush the scilla off? Pick out your best pattern of movement and practise it.

2. Practise in small groups being pulled towards a central point. What happens when all meet? Is there any sound? Practise your sounds to fit them.
3. How do you think the scilla would move? Get a good starting position and move as you think they would.
(Sounds by teacher again to produce soft rolling, unwinding and exploding, jerky convulsions and crack, with rhythms of great variety on tambour, drum, cymbal.)
Make your own noises before, during, and after your movement.
Is the noise the same throughout?
How do you pull your victim along?
With which part of your body are you in contact with your victim?
Change this and alter your pulling movement to fit it.
Do you try to entwine them?
4. Practise being:
   a. Soldiers firing at the sea tanks. Move about as you think they would to get the best position.
   b. The priest.
   c. The people. Think clearly how you are going to react. Are you going to hide, to barricade yourself in, to attack the thing, to shelter with the priest? Perhaps you are caught under falling masonry or pulled away from it?
   Work in pairs to develop the scene with the tanks from different points of view.
   a. Rescuer and rescued, ever aware of the tanks.
   b. Man and wife.
   c. Two children.
   d. Parents who have lost children.
   e. Children who have lost parents.
   Talk it over first and then act out your reaction to the tanks. After suitable practice this could evolve into a class drama.

The Iron Man

1. Be the Iron Man:
   happily eating the metal in the scrap-yard
   following Hogarth's tapping
   searching for another part of your body

         getting hotter and hotter during the challenge
         moving towards the edge of the cliff
         waiting for Hogarth's father's car to come, as it is driven at you.
         (The signal means that your foot has been knocked off. Show what
         happens.)

2. Make a machine shape with your body. Be sure what your machine does
and where each part is.

On a signal a part of the machine is bitten off by the Iron Man. Show
your shape now. Repeat this several times.

Get in a group. Each of you is to take up a farm machine shape. The
Iron Man is to come through the farmyard biting parts off the machines.
Talk it over first to decide where and what you will be, and the order
in which you are bitten. Alter your shapes and hold them still when you
hear the signal. Can you make some part of your machine shape show
the impressions of the Iron Man's teeth?

3. Be:

         the people picnicking on the hill
         the soldiers attacking the Space Being
         the farmers digging the pit and disguising it
         the people taking the Iron Man apart
         the people building the grid of girders
         the farmers leading the Iron Man to the scrap-yard.

4. You are Hogarth trapping the Iron Man. Practise making a tapping
sound. Move about making your sound and luring the Iron Man towards
the pit.

Get in a good position for his final steps.

Show how you feel when the Iron Man is in the hole.

5. You are going to work as a class on the story up to when the Iron Man
is in the scrap-yard.

Decide which scenes of the story you are going to act out.

Decide where each scene is to take place.

Decide how you are going to link the scenes together.

Act through the scenes.

Written work

1. 'But that was nothing to what ...' ('Welsh Incident') Begin with this
and develop your own ideas in verse form. Think carefully of the end
as your story unfolds.

2. Collect some pictures of space, or space travel, from the newspapers and magazines. Weave a story around them using the pictures you have collected as illustrations of your story.
3. You were on the beach at Criccieth ('Welsh Incident'). Tell what happened.
4. What do you think would be happening in the town of Criccieth next day? Write an account as if you were a visitor to the town.
5. Tell the story of the 'Welsh Incident' from the points of view of the 'things'.
   Give yourselves good fitting names.
   What was your purpose?
   Was it the first time you had done this sort of thing?
   How did you prepare for it?
   What did it feel like coming into this new place?
   Were you used to it?
   Listen again to the poem 'Tea in a Space Ship'. Was that what you were used to? If so, how did the new surroundings surprise you?
   What was your reception?
6. Prepare a report for the creatures back home of the things you saw and heard when you came out of the sea. What things might a 'creature' find strange that we take for granted: a band playing, a telephone kiosk, the houses?
7. 'If I were invisible . . .'. Tell about the things you would like to do if you were really invisible, and sure no one could see you and blame you for it afterwards.
8. Write about what you did and how you felt when you were Hogarth leading the Iron Man to the pit.
9. You are at the challenge. Write about what happened.
10. What do you think the beginning of *The Iron Man* tells us about the importance of *each part* of your body?
11. In *The Iron Man* it says his head was 'as big as a bedroom'—yet a seagull lifted his ear. What do you think of this?
12. Write ten words that could describe the Iron Man. Try to shape them into a poem.

Index of Books

Fiction

Esther Hautzig	*The Endless Steppe*	Penguin (Peacock Book)
Maurice Herzog	*Annapurna*	Collins (Fontana Books)
Barry Hines	*Kes (A Kestrel for a Knave)*	Penguin
Helen Hoke (ed.)	*Witches, Witches, Witches*	Chatto and Windus
J. Hope-Simpson	*The Hamish Hamilton Book of Witches*	Hamish Hamilton
W. H. Hudson	*A Shepherd's Life*	Dent (Everyman)
Richard Hughes	*A High Wind in Jamaica*	Penguin
Ted Hughes	*How the Whale Became*	Faber
Ted Hughes	*The Iron Man*	Faber
Tom Ingram	*The Hungry Cloud*	Collins
Jerome K. Jerome	*Three Men in a Boat*	Penguin
Erich Kästner	*Emil and the Detectives*	Puffin
Clive King	*Stig of the Dump*	Puffin
Clive King	*The 22 Letters*	Puffin
Eleanor Frances Lattimore	*The Little Tumbler*	Angus and Robertson
Laurie Lee	*Cider with Rosie*	Penguin
Doris Lessing	*The Habit of Loving*	MacGibbon and Kee
C. Day Lewis	*The Otterbury Incident*	Puffin
C. S. Lewis	*The Lion, the Witch, and the Wardrobe*	Puffin
Eric Linklater	*The Wind on the Moon*	Macmillan
N. L. Lloyd and G. Palmer (eds.)	*Journey by Broomstick*	Odhams
Jack London	*Call of the Wild*	Heinemann (New Windmill series)
Konrad Z. Lorenz	*King Solomon's Ring*	Methuen
W. Mankowitz	*A Kid for Two Farthings*	Andre Deutsch
Ruth Manning-Sanders	*Circus Boy*	O.U.P.
Ruth Manning-Sanders (ed.)	*Red Indian Folk and Fairy Tales*	O.U.P.
John Masefield	*Jim Davis*	Puffin
Gavin Maxwell	*Ring of Bright Water*	Pan
William Mayne	*A Swarm in May*	O.U.P.
William Mayne	*No More School*	Puffin
William Mayne	*Pig in the Middle*	Puffin
William Mayne	*Plot Night*	Puffin
William Mayne	*Sand*	Puffin
Michael Mott	*Master Entrick*	Puffin

Louise Jean Walker (ed).	*Red Indian Legends*	Odhams
John Walsh	*The House in the Cedar Tree*	Heinemann
Keith Waterhouse	*There is a Happy Land*	Penguin
Ronald Welch	*Knight Crusader*	O.U.P.
H.G. Wells	*Kipps*	Collins
H.G. Wells	*The Invisible Man*	Collins
H.G. Wells	*War of the Worlds*	Penguin
T.H. White	*The Goshawk*	Penguin
T.H. White	*The Sword in the Stone*	Collins
Laura Ingalls Wilder	*Little House in the Big Woods*	Puffin
Laura Ingalls Wilder	*The Long Winter*	Puffin
J.H. Williams	*Bandoola*	Penguin
John Wyndham	*The Kraken Wakes*	Penguin
John Wyndham	*The Midwich Cuckoos*	Penguin

Poetry

In alphabetical order of book title:

The Albemarle Book of Modern Verse 1, 2	ed. F.E.S Finn	John Murray
All Day Long	ed. Pamela Whitlock	O.U.P.
American Poetry. An Introductory Anthology	ed. Donald Hall	Faber
An Anthology of Free Verse	ed. James Reeves	Blackwell
As Large as Alone	ed. C. Copeman and J. Gibson	Macmillan
The Ballad of the Kon-Tiki and other verses	Ian Serraillier	O.U.P.
Birds, Beasts, and Fishes	ed. Ruth Manning-Sanders	O.U.P.
Birthright Poetry 1—4	ed. W.T. Cunningham	Hamish Hamilton
Blackwell's Junior Poetry Books 1—4	ed. Evan Owen	Blackwell
The Book of a Thousand Poems	ed. J. Murray MacBain	Evans
The Children's Bells	Eleanor Farjeon	O.U.P.
A Choice of Whitman's Verse	ed. Donald Hall	Faber (paperback)
Collected Poems	A.E. Housman	Penguin
Collected Poems	Louis MacNeice	Faber
Collected Poems	Stephen Spender	Faber

Old Possum's Book of Practical Cats	T.S. Eliot	Faber
Other Men's Flowers	ed. A.P. Wavell	Jonathan Cape
The Oxford Book of Poetry for Children	ed. Edward Blishen	O.U.P.
The Oxford Book of Verse for Juniors	ed. James Britton	O.U.P.
The Pattern of Poetry	ed. William Kean Seymour and John Smith	Burke
Pegasus 1—5	ed. Nora Grisenthwaite	Schofield and Sims
The Penguin Book of Animal Verse	ed. George Macbeth	Penguin
The Penguin Book of Contemporary Verse	ed. Kenneth Allott	Penguin
Penguin New Poetry	ed. A. Alvarez	Penguin
The Pilgrim Book of Verse 1, 2		Grant
Poetry and Life 1—4	ed. Nora Grisenthwaite	Schofield and Sims
Poetry Panorama 1—4	ed. H. Perry	Odhams
A Puffin Quartet of Poets	ed. E. Graham	Penguin
Rhyme and Reason	ed. Raymond O'Malley and Denys Thompson	Chatto and Windus
Rhyme and Rhythm	ed. J. Gibson and R. Wilson	Macmillan
Round the Day	ed. Rumer Godden	Macmillan
Round the Year	ed. Rumer Godden	Macmillan
The Roundabout by the Sea	John Walsh	O.U.P.
Selected Poems	Robert Frost	Penguin
Selected Poems	Robert Graves	Penguin
Selected Poems	Miroslav Holub	Penguin
Selected Poems	D.H. Lawrence	Penguin
Selected Poems	Stevie Smith	Longman
Silver-Sand and Snow	Eleanor Farjeon	Michael Joseph
Song at the Year's Turning	R.S. Thomas	Hart-Davis
The Song of Hiawatha	H.W. Longfellow	Dent
The Sphere of Glass	John Lehmann	Hogarth Press
This Way Delight	ed. Herbert Read	Faber
Thoughtshapes	ed. Barry Maybury	O.U.P.
Twentieth Century Poetry	ed. Harold Monro	Chatto and Windus

On teaching

Randolph Quirk	*The Use of English*	Longman, 1962
James Reeves	*Teaching Poetry*	Heinemann, 1963
G.R. Roberts and V. Southgate	*Reading: Which Approach?*	U.L.P., 1970
V. Southgate and F.W. Warburton	*I.T.A.: An Independent Evaluation*	John Murray and W. and R. Chambers, 1969
Brian Way	*Development through Drama*	Longman, 1967
Ruth H. Weir	*Language in the Crib*	Mouton, 1962
Andrew Wilkinson	*The Foundations of Language*	O.U.P., 1971
	Children's Literature in Education	Ward Lock Educational (quarterly)
	Drama—Educational Survey 2	H.M.S.O., 1968
	Language	H.M.S.O., 1951